LIVERPOOL LOG BOOK

RICHARD WHITTINGTON-EGAN

THE GALLERY PRESS
LEIGHTON ROAD, NESTON, SOUTH WIRRAL

ISBN 0 900389 28 1
Published by Gallery Press 1987

Printed by Scotprint (North West) Limited.

The Liverpool Dossier Series
All titles in this series were originally published in Richard Whittington-Egan's earlier books LIVERPOOL COLONNADE and LIVERPOOL ROUNDABOUT.

Now available:–

Dossier 1. Tales of Liverpool: Murder, Mayhem and Mystery.

Dossier 2. Liverpool Characters and Eccentrics.

Dossier 3. Liverpool Ghosts and Ghouls.

Dossier 4. Liverpool Oddities.

Dossier 5. The Great Liverpool Blitz.

Dossier 6. Liverpool Log Book.

Back in the days when the Beatles would still pop into Ye Cracke in Rice Street to take a friendly ale with me, I was paying a young man's court to the fickle jade of the Mersey. I wrote two love chronicles of our on-off affair—*Liverpool Colonnade* and *Liverpool Roundabout.* Oh, I was a knight-errant then, pricking in fancy my milk-white palfrey through the stone forest and down the avenues of my imagination. And such imaginings! I saw the the Liver birds take wing against a low lying hunter's moon . . . the chimney-masted tangle of sky-riding roof-tops looking at dusk like the decks of ships at swaying anchor . . . I heard the golden and porcelained names on windows singing the old crafts' songs and lullabies of trade . . . I lurked around the Western bazaar counters in the lit grottoes of the shops . . . I rode the overhead railway and the Noah's Ark tramcars . . . watched the glittering city slip over the horizon's edge into the purple pomp of night—and out again into the watered-milk light of another dawn. Both I and the Liverpool of which I wrote have grown up, grown different. We have played weather-vanes to the wind of change. And yet we are still the same at heart. The fresh wind blowing across the river and over my city's wild hilltop still whispers the old tales to those who are willing to listen . . . a light still burns in Paradise Street . . .

CONTENTS

		Page
1	Taxi	7
2	Punch Takes a Blow	10
3	Coffee and Culture	13
4	Behind the Scenes	15
5	There is Sweet Music Here	18
6	Children Off the Streets	21
7	Willingly to School	24
8	Half-Day with the Muses	26
9	Readers' Retreat	29
10	Olympian Ghosts	31
11	An Old Master	33
12	After the Dustcart . . .	36
13	The Pipes of Pan and the Serpent	39
14	Jazz Waves of the Merseysippi	41
15	The Inside Story of Liverpool's Big Ben	43
16	The Fabulous National	47
17	A Poet in Dockland	53
18	The Amateur Gunman	55
19	Cosseting the Calder Stones	60

1. TAXI!

A green wooden hut in the centre of Williamson Square is the most exclusive café in Liverpool. It bears no sign, nothing to identify it as an eating house. I don't suppose one person in a thousand has passed through its little green door, for this is Liverpool's last surviving cabman's shelter and in order to qualify for admittance you must be a taxi driver.

One evening recently I knocked at that small door. It was opened by Mrs. Farrimond who for nearly twenty years now has been catering for Liverpool's hungry cabbies. When I had explained to her that I wanted to meet some of the men who drive the city's taxis, she led me into a large square room and sat me down with a cup of tea at a long oilcloth-covered table round which a dozen or so taxi drivers were busy addressing themselves to huge plates of liver and bacon.

Once upon a time a visit to a cabman's shelter was an essential ingredient of a real night out. In the days of the Edwardian swells many a reveller, homeward-bound from one of those glittering parties of a vanished age, would plead for a plate of bacon and eggs or toad-in-the-hole for himself and the lovely lady on his arm. Nor was it only stage-door Johnnies with their pretty prizes from the chorus who sat down eagerly to sausage and mash in such places. In a certain shelter hard by London's Green Park, and known far and wide as the Junior Turf Club, you could regularly meet famous men like the poet, Ernest Dowson, and Sir Ernest Shackleton, the explorer, and, cheek-by-jowl with ravenous down-and-outs, gay young sprigs of the nobility. It is even whispered that from time to time the bearded face of a certain Royal Prince might be glimpsed there quaffing a cup of coffee that could not be found in a palace at 3 a.m.

★ ★ ★ ★

But all that is changed now. The midnight sausage has been outlawed, and to-day the cabbies' shelter has no visitors. It is a great pity because the cabby off duty is a character worth knowing. I could scarcely credit that those witty laughing men I met round Mrs. Farrimond's table were the austere figures behind whom I have so often sat in their black leather taxis. Until then, the man at the wheel had always been something of an enigma to me. I never really considered him as a human being. He was a back seen through a window – a hunched back expressing boredom or irritability, an erect back signifying alertness, even cockiness, but just a back. Sometimes I noticed his hat, whether it was a battered trilby or a smart peaked-cap. But mostly I accepted him almost as a part of his machine and only began to endow him with individuality when I started to think about how much I ought to tip him.

Now I know quite a bit about his natural history. I know that there are 300 taxis in Liverpool which operate from 102 stands, excluding those at the three main railway stations. I know that a taxi costs £1,012 to buy and that its life is exactly 11 years. I have learned that a taximeter must be bought separately, and that as it costs £55 many drivers prefer to hire one at the rate of 3s. a week. I have visited the Hackney Carriage Office in Hood Street where, before he is issued with one of the coveted metal badges, every candidate must pass an eyesight test, a special driving test and a very tough examination as to the whereabouts of city and suburban streets, principal buildings, hospitals, places of entertainment, docks, clubs and the quickest routes between various points.

★ ★ ★ ★

It was in Williamson Square, however, that I got to know the men themselves a cheery humorous crowd, as they sat yarning with me by the gas-fire in the shelter.

"If I was to write a book about my experiences *Alice in Wonderland* wouldn't compare with it," Mr. Arthur Stanley Schofield, who has been 44 years a Liverpool cabby, told me. "This job is an education in itself, you meet the best and the worst."

"Pal of mine met a couple of the worst the other night," chimed in a driver at the far end of the table. "Two chaps stopped his cab and told him to drive to Cazneau Street. When they got there they refused to pay the fare and did a bunk. Old Charlie ups and out and chases them. A policeman with one of those Alsatians happened to be standing nearby and saw the whole thing. He let the dog go and it caught Charlie."

"Aye, you get some right queer customers," said the driver they called 'Have-a-Go' (cabbies, by the way, are great ones for nicknames). "A few years back there was a fellow who used to set two dogs on you as soon as you got to his house, and there was another bloke who always wanted to fight you for the fare money."

Not that there is always difficulty over getting the fare. One driver met a man off the Irish boat and drove him to an address in the suburbs. At the end of the journey the man handed the cabby a boot-box. He opened it and inside was £400 in one-pound notes. A few months later that driver met the Irish boat again and could hardly believe his eyes when he saw his previous benefactor hurrying down the gangway. Once again he drove him out to the house in the suburbs, and once again a boot-box was produced. The fare opened the box himself this time and, dividing its contents in half, handed the astonished cabby £250.

Then there was the story of the taxi cruising along Church Street when a middle-aged man signalled it, said "Hamburg," and jumped in. "Hamburg?" echoed the bewildered driver. "Yes, Hamburg, Germany," and off they went on what was surely the longest trip of any Liverpool taxi. The shortest, maybe, was that of a lady who hailed a cab in Lime Street at a quarter to four one afternoon and shouted, "Quick, I've got to be in Buckingham Palace by four o'clock." "Sorry, lady, I don't think I'll be able to make it by four," said the alarmed cabby, and off he drove as fast as his wheels would take him to pull himself together over a strong cup of tea in Williamson Square!

2. PUNCH TAKES A BLOW

The year 1957 broke over Liverpool somewhat sadly.

The very night preceding that on which the hooters and sirens proclaimed its birth, saw the last train crash and rumble, to the fluttering of damp handkerchiefs, along the waterfront sky-line of the 63-year-old Overhead Railway. Within the first few weeks of the New Year, far from unmourned, world-famous old Paddy's Market received its death sentence, and it was confirmed that the last remnants of the Goree Piazzas were scheduled for destruction. Liverpool, it seemed, was determined to lose – not so much lose, perhaps, as voluntarily sacrifice – a great deal of its character. Bitterly, one reflected that it only remained to blow up St. George's Hall, knock down the Royal Liver Building, raze the Cathedral, demolish the Town Hall, and erect some of those hideous tower blocks of flats on their sites, to ensure the maintenance of that reputation for progressive vandalism which this city has so well and truly earned.

It was at this point that one of the cruellest blows of all fell. Poor old Mr. Punch who, per the 'Professors' Codman – four generations of them – had for the last 130 years delighted thousands of children and their elders at Number One Lime Street, was suddenly condemned to banishment. Early in January the town-clerk was given authority, pursuant to the Highways Committee's decision that obstructions in busy streets must go, to "secure the removal from the highway before February 1st, 1957, of the Punch and Judy show standing at the junction of Lime Street and St. George's Place." The trouble was that the site of 'Professor' Codman's castello was bang in the centre of a proposed car park which is a vital part of the city's new one-way traffic plan. Of course logic and all the forces of law and order stood arraigned on the side of the Liverpool City Council, and 60-year-old puppeteer, Richard Codman, entered the lists with sentiment as his only henchman. But it is well not to underestimate the power of sentiment. Like faith it has been known to move mountains before now. And as for logic, well we English can be obstinately illogical when the fancy takes us. National crises have often been sparked by very tiny issues, as witness the case of George Archer-Shee – the real-life 'Winslow Boy' – who fought the big guns of the British navy to establish his innocence on a charge of the theft of five shillings . . . and won.

★ ★ ★ ★

Strictly speaking, Mr. Punch is an interloper in Liverpool. He is an alien, but not, I think, an undesirable one. Born *Pulcinella* – a name which very likely derives from *pulcino,* the Italian for a chicken, and hence the preposterous 'beak' and chirrupy voice – in Naples somewhere about the end of the 16th century, his ancestral stock probably harks back to Attic Greece and Imperial Rome. Certainly, some of the masks and figures of the ancient Roman pantomime – Maccus, Bucco and Cicurrus, for instance – bear more than a passing resemblance, both of aspect and attitude, to our more familiar Punch. In his cradle days *Pulcinella* was a carnival-mask character of the Neapolitan *commedia dell' arte,* and it was not until some years later that he found new life as a marionette.

It was during the 17th century that *Pulcinella* crossed the border into France, changing his name in transit to *Polichinelle,* and hence he sailed across the Channel, reaching England, as Punch, about the time of Charles II.

His welcome here was enthusiastic. Before long the irrepressible Sam Pepys was writing in his diary, "To *Polichinelli* at Charing Cross which is prettier and prettier and so full of variety that it is extra-ordinarily good entertainment." And his appreciation was echoed by Addison and Steele, Swift and Gay, and Hogarth and Fielding.

Towards the middle of the 18th century Punch discarded his white Italian dress, and with it he shed his original character of comedian, hen-pecked husband and receiver of life's slaps, to become the amiably sinister wag, the wife-beater and universal assassin that we know. By 1880 he had been transformed from a string into a glove or sleeve puppet, and had also quit the puppet-theatre proper in favour of the castello or portable booth. Mr. Punch had, in other words, gone on the street.

And it is as part of the street scene that we think of him. In rain and shine his gay-striped booth brings colour to the slaty pavements. His beacon burns through the grey, gas-lit streets of Victorian England, brilliant as the naphtha flares that lightened the drizzling darkness where the throng huddled about the little canvas frame. He belongs to Dickens and to Mayhew, and yet he also belongs to us. The old iconoclast still goes through his preordained paces with Judy, Dog Toby, the baby, the policeman, Joey the clown, the boxers, the demon, the skeleton, the crocodile and Jack Ketch the hangman.

★ ★ ★ ★

To-day there are not so many Punch and Judy shows left. Liverpool is – I hope I shall never have to write *was* – the only city in England which can boast the permanent presence of one in its streets. Our 'Professor' Codman's show is an institution – a part of Liverpool. You will find it officially recognised in the guide-books and marked on the maps. You will come upon it unexpectedly in the pages of such Liverpool novels as John Brophy's *City of Departures.*

Thirty-five years ago the citizens of Liverpool subscribed to a brand-new booth, which was presented to Mr. Codman by the Sandon Studios Society in the forecourt of Liberty Building. It was quite an occasion, with the Liverpool City Police Band in attendance. I could not believe that those same citizens would allow the 'Professor' and his little company of immortals to be banished from their streets.

It was a worried Mr. Codman who greeted me when I stepped behind his 200-year-old proscenium with its crusting of finely-carved wooden heads made out of driftwood by Richard Codman primus to decorate his caravan. "I had hoped that my son Ronald would carry on the family tradition in Liverpool," he told me. "After all, ever since my great-grandfather came here from Llandudo and set up his booth we Codmans have given shows on this self-same spot. It is home to us."

I gathered that he was determined to fight for his four-foot stake of Liverpool earth, and as I left him preparing for the next performance I hoped that the city fathers would remember the children who love to stand wide-eyed before his bright little booth watching Mr. Punch, his long-suffering wife, Dog Toby and all the rest going through their age-old antics. It would, I felt, be unthinkable to let those crimson curtains be rung down on three and a half centuries of history and 130 years of childhood delight in Liverpool.

POST SCRIPTUM

In the event, sentiment it was that, quite properly, won the day.

Both national and local press took up cudgels on Mr. Punch's behalf. Sackfuls of letters deluged the newspaper offices, petitions were organised, thousands of voices cried loud in protest and a new pitch was found for 'Professor' Codman on nearby St. George's Plateau.

So it came about that, in its 750th Charter Year, Liverpool made a gracious gesture for which thousands of yet unborn children will bless it.

3. COFFEE AND CULTURE

When, with shops shuttered and the staccato chatter of legions of office typewriters silenced, evening closes in on workaday Liverpool, there opens, like some exotic night-flowering blossom, a certain Bohemian club which is the Mecca of noctambulant artistic Liverpool.

This club, appropriately quartered in the attic reaches of an out-of-the-way city building within a stone's throw of the Bold Street atelier where once the young August John painted pictures that nobody wanted to buy, is approached by a twisting stone stairway, and the other evening I climbed its 44 worn steps and found myself, albeit somewhat breathless, in the red-painted portrait-hung room where, any evening between 9 o'clock and midnight, you can see the Bohemians at play.

★ ★ ★ ★

"Coffee or tea?" inquired the proprietress as I seated myself at the small table with its neat gingham cloth. Bohemia, it would seem, has gone soft – at any rate in the matter of drinks. In my day it was the bar-counter that provided platform for the egoism of inexperience. To-day, the embryo artist and his hangers-on take coffee with their culture. And very good coffee it is, accompanied if you wish by choice morsels of continental fare.

Lingering there over my *café noir,* I watched the little cliques forgather. Young girls, self-consciously svelte in tapered black trousers, immoderately curved in tight wool sweaters, barbarically resplendent with dangling Zingari ear-hoops, puffing contemptuous smoke from infinitely long cigarette-holders into the wincing face of convention. Youths, aggressively self-satisfied, in rainbow scarves and drab corduroys, displaying tangled heads of unkept hair together with the occasional rash of scrawny beard, vying with one another in loudly-voiced attempts to impress their intense, and intensely female, audience.

All these young people seemed to see themselves as the lineal descendants of Murger's Rodolphe and Mimi, and this colourful corner of Liverpool is nightly transformed for them into the equivalent of a Parisian *bistro.* "Art's the thing," they will tell you. And so it is, viewed with a full stomach and the knowledge of a warm bed beneath the parental roof at Childwall. But there is the difference between appearance and reality upon which latter-day art insist. It is all very well to look like an artist, even to play at being an artist, but – what of the reality? The discovery that art may be, as Scott remarked of writing, "an excellent walking-stick, but a poor crutch"? What of the unwilling awakening to the fact that except for the few, the very few, a career in art may lead to starving in a garret – not at all a romantic proceeding when you actually come to do it – or a gradual drifting into what is slightingly identified as 'commercial art'? It compels no crystal to prophecy the bitter disappointment that is to accompany a future failure to translate fiery ideals into cold cash.

But for the moment, that living present which is all-important when one is young, there is at least the satisfaction of talk, and coffee is only sixpence a cup! And so they go on discussing with painful earnestness the contents of this or that little review, conspicuously upturned amidst the half-empty cups. Whilst about them, like faded moths attracted to the quick flame of youth, circles a little cloud of older men and women. Their motives need not be suspect. They are only seeking to recapture by bright association with the young something of which the years have robbed them. It is a foolish conceit and it is very, very sad.

★ ★ ★ ★

Strident young voices clamouring for attention break in upon one's thoughts. All the posturing and posing irritate you . . . and yet . . . inevitably, they recall something of yourself, something that you had thought long since dead. For a moment you hesitate, the smile that springs to your lips at all this make-believe is tinged with a suspicion of wistfulness and a nagging regret tugs briefly at your sleeve as you descend the stairs and walk back into the street, back into whatever life and the years have made you since, far-away and long-ago, you too pondered the eternal verities and refashioned the world just as these young folk are doing to-day.

4. BEHIND THE SCENES

"QUIET ROOM" said the notice on the door, but that is not precisely how I would have described it. Even before I had pushed my way through, strident voices could be heard struggling for mastery on the other side.

Within, the room was bare; a platform at one end, a piano in the corner, a dozen people seated in creaking wickerwork chairs. A rather worried-looking young man sat at a small green table, making notes on little white cards, while three young men in blazers and flannels, and a girl in a dirndl skirt and ballerina shoes, stood shouting and gesticulating before him. The young man at the table stubbed out his cigarette in the high-piled ash-tray. "All right, break," he said. "That took exactly forty minutes and was quite good."

Such was my introduction to a rehearsal of Christopher Fry's "The Lady's not for Burning" which the Masque Players were busy licking into shape for an open-air production which was to take place in Calderstones Park.

The traditional call, "Beginners, please," had sounded at 7.30 p.m. and, fresh from their offices and shops, eight men and three women with theatre in their blood had hurried to this unquiet quiet room to go through their paces as spare time actors and actresses. In some ways it is a difficult thing to explain, this zest for the footlights that drives doctors, solicitors, accountants, shop assistants, schoolteachers, librarians and civil servants to the abandonment of their leisure. Mostly, they do it purely and simply because they like it – or so they told me – but it is hard work. Not only are there lines to be learned, mumbling fervently to oneself in streets and on bus tops until one acquires the reputation of mild eccentricity, but long hours must be spent 'getting inside' the character to be portrayed, translating the sparse delineation of a script's cold print into the warm and breathing actuality of a convincing personality on stage. Then, all the weeks of painstaking rehearsal; the integrating of individual interpretations; the repeating of phrases and sentences over and over again, until at length they cease to have any meaning and ring hollowly in the ears, disembodied sense-divorced patterns of sound. And, finally, what does it all add up to? A couple of hours on the night with, perhaps, four or five repeat performances.

★ ★ ★ ★

"Right everyone, break for tea," shouted the producer, and we climbed up so many flights of stairs to the canteen that I spent the rest of the evening wondering how anyone managed to have breath enough left to say their lines.

Over a cup of tea and a cigarette I chatted with various members of the company. The first spare time actor I met was Paul Frayne, a young schoolmaster who was playing the lead. He contrived to look extraordinarily like Christopher Fry and brought considerable sensitivity to his interpretation of Thomas Mendip, a discharged soldier whose chief desire in life is to lose it through a hangman's noose. This pedagogic note was maintained by the female lead, Joan Paton, also a school-teacher, who as Jennet Jourdemayne, the life-clinging damsel who is a most unwilling candidate for the fire stakes, gave evidence of having learned her theatrical lessons well. Another gracefully talented member of the cast was 25-year-old Pamela Barnes. During the day this young woman hides her light beneath the overall of an assistant in a city music shop. Her leisure is devoted to acting, singing and painting. As a painter she has had some success, having, so she told me, sold a picture only a week or two before. A mezzosoprano, she has ambitions towards opera, and confided that the rôle she most covets is that of Carmen, but she would be quite prepared to settle for Carmen Jones! Acting, however, is her first love, and throughout eight years of amateur activity she has kept a steady eye on the celluloid Mecca of the films.

★ ★ ★ ★

"Act Three, beginners," said the producer in loud business-like tones, and down we all trooped to the quiet room again. The schoolmaster took the stage, where he was joined by a doctor, who confessed himself an extrovert who had got into the habit of acting at school and university and now found it a relaxing relief from the cabined confines of the consulting room, and a legal gentleman who revelled in this brief respite from briefs. The inevitable lady with the knitting, who had made great progress during the earlier part of the evening, relapsed into her basket-chair and started with renewed fervour upon the equally inevitable scarf. Once more the voices echoed in that bare, brown, boarded room, their words contrasting most oddly with the modern clothes of the mummers and the undraped austerity of their background.

At 10 o'clock the curtain – if curtain there had been – had to come down on the little world of mediaeval make-believe, as the room was required for other purposes, and the rehearsal dissolved into a confusion of talk in which I caught snatches of reference to flex, recording machines, 5-amp. plugs and suchlike unmediaeval objects of off-stagecraft. There was also a good deal of telling criticism by the producer, and the lady prompter was desperately calling for volunteers to load a prop van at New Brighton before 9 a.m. the following morning a cue which was not taken up with any marked enthusiasm! "Remember, dress rehearsal 9 a.m. Sunday," admonished the producer stuffing his sheaves of papers into a brief-case. And, one-by-one, the players, assuring one another that it would be "all right on the night," slipped out to tell their fifteenth-century lines over again to the twentieth-century stars.

5. THERE IS SWEET MUSIC HERE

Seven-thirty on a Saturday night.

The bright-coloured top that is town beginning to spin.

Queues of those who like to purchase their pleasure ready-made line the twinkling streets and curl about the cinemas and theatres.

In restaurant and public-house thousands of others are busying themselves forging their own more personal fun.

Up the dark slope of Hardman Street, insulated within the clean-lined brick building that crests the hill, 1,900 music-loving Merseysiders voyage happily on a sea of sound.

Beyond those walls the Saturday-night town hums, but it is here in the Philharmonic Hall that the real music of Liverpool is played – now louder than the roar of all the city's traffic, now soft as the whisper of waves picking the old sea-wall.

I sit in the stalls and let my eyes wander. Away from the platform with its black-and-white patina of musicians, ranged like chessmen, its stained wood and shining brass; away from the weaving baton, conducting and controlling in the maestro's hand, my gaze steals furtively along the quiet, rapt rows. Here a young face flushed with discovery; there an old face tranquil with remembrance. An elderly lady leans back in her seat with closed eyes. A young man with unruly hair is bent forward over the open score on his lap. Two teenage girls sit clasping hands, their lips slightly apart. And all around and about us the music, stirring as many responsive chords as there are listeners in the audience.

★ ★ ★ ★

For 108 years now there has been music at the top of Hardman Street, for it was in August 1849 that the Liverpool Philharmonic Society, which had been founded nine years previously by a group of Liverpool gentlemen with the avowed intention of co-ordinating and extending musical interests in the city, opened its first concert hall on the site of the present Philharmonic Hall.

In the early days concerts were much longer than they are to-day. Glancing through some of the old programmes I saw that it was by no means unusual for the first half alone to include an overture, a concerto and a full symphony, together with a liberal sprinkling of arias, the entire performance occupying anything up to four hours. Nowadays, a concert generally lasts about two hours, and that includes an interval for the taking of coffee or maybe something stronger.

There have been other changes, too. Once upon a time no-one would be admitted to a concert unless wearing full evening-dress. From where I was sitting I could see a number of men in sports jackets and flannels and at least three young women in slacks.

It may have been because at this point the music suddenly took on a mood of savage grandeur, that I found myself wondering how many twentieth-century concert-goers realise that every time they go to listen to music they are assisting at a rite which is almost as old as man himself.

Experts estimate that for fully 25,000 years men and women have surrendered themselves to the pleasure of patterned sound. Music began in the jungle and the swamp, and though it is a long stretch from the first drums and rattles used in ancient fertility rites and primitive obsequies to sun and moon, to the euphonious and highly skilled music of modern times, basic principles have changed little. The thunder of Beethoven, the complex melodic threads of Bach and the bucolic gaiety of Haydn all depend upon the blowing, scraping and banging of wood, bone, metal, goat-skins, sheep's guts and bits of bamboo. There is indeed something ageless about music. It diminishes space and time as no other art can. Its melodies stem from every country. Its listeners are often tuned in to wavelengths of sound created a couple of hundred years ago. This quality of timelessness is emphasised by the very structure of the new Philharmonic Hall, which in 1939 replaced the old hall, burned down in July 1933, for, incredibly, the entire shell of the auditorium is suspended in space, slung from the roof of the outer building. Moreoever, the atmosphere within that shell is most definitely timeless for, entirely without windows, it excludes the external world of day and night.

★ ★ ★ ★

It was in the greenroom that, during the interval, I was shown two great leather-bound volumes between whose covers is preserved a large slice of the history of what is among the half-dozen oldest musical societies in the world. These books are crammed with a series of photographs, many of them signed with fading fanfares of eccentric copperplate, of the musically great who have graced our city with their artistry – Jenny Lind, Paderewski, Melba, Tetrazzini, Patti and a host of others. It was not without a certain pride that I discovered on the very first page of the first volume a photograph of my own great-grandfather, James Zeugheer-Herrmann, the Philharmonic Society's first resident conductor.

But it is not as a museum, nor even because of the excellence of the coffee that one can drink there, that the greenroom is important. It is because of the lively part which it plays in the cultural life of Liverpool. There, on concert nights, guests from many different professions and branches of art and commerce are invited to meet one another and be introduced to the conductor and the artists.

It was just after 9.30 when the concert finished. Out into the night and down the hill spilled the audience. As I watched them go they seemed a strangely-assorted crowd. Now and again I caught a snatch of conversation. "But, my dear, Tchaikovsky's Fifth – it's HEAVEN. You simply *must* know it." "Well, darling, personally I just *adore* Mozart," Some spoke just a semitone too loudly, but on the whole I am sure that they were sincere enough. I am sure, too, that each and every one of them appreciated to the full the magic of music – that strange power it has of transporting our own little sufferings into the realms of majestic tragedy and setting a seal of greatness upon our equally insignificant triumphs.

6. CHILDREN OFF THE STREETS

Take the noisiest afternoon in the parrot house at the zoo, add the uproar of the lion house at feeding time, mix in the howls of a troop of excited baboons for good measure, and you have some idea of what it is like on a quiet night at Liverpool's Rodney Youth Centre.

As I followed Miss Stella Baker, the warden, into the large main hall of the 93-year-old gymnasium in Myrtle Street, which has been called, "a street corner with a roof on," the sound of 150 of Liverpool's children-with-nowhere-else-to-go at play, struck my ears with something like the impact of the roar of the Minotaur.

"I'm afraid you've chosen a rather quiet evening," Miss Baker shouted above the din. "You see this is the first night we've been open after the summer break."

I was about to reply, when a small girl who had been climbing, like an embryo Ann Bonny, up a scrambling net, suddenly leapt on my back, and another infant came hurtling round the corner and darted between my legs. I was just getting my breath back when a football thudded past my head and hit the wall behind me with a resounding thwack. "Sorry, Guv," yelled a bright-eyed nine-year-old who looked pathetically aged in a pair of tattered long trousers.

"You're all right. They've taken to you," said Miss Baker. I'm glad she told me! "If they hadn't," she added, "you would quite likely have had your shins well kicked by now and probably something would have dropped on you – by accident you understand – from the gallery."

Make no mistake, although the habitués of the Rodney Youth Centre are all between the ages of 5 and 21, it is probably one of the toughest places on Merseyside, and the wonder of it is that a small mousy-haired woman has for the past fourteen years coped successfully with an undertaking which, prior to her taking it on, had, in just over six months, broken the hearts of a couple of male wardens.

It was in 1939 that the centre was started by a group of men and women who had the unattached youth of Merseyside on their consciences.

It first opened its doors at the old Wellington Assembly-Rooms in Mount Pleasant, once the venue of fashionable Liverpool, where it functioned simply as a dance-hall for teenagers.

Six months later it was blitzed and had to close down. A year was to elapse before once again it came to life.

It remained open for precisely one week, at the end of which time the warden resigned in despair. Eventually, another warden was found to take on the job. He lasted six months before he, too, gave up the ghost. It was at this juncture that Miss Baker came upon the scene.

In the early days at Mount Pleasant, the main problem was to create an atmosphere that would attract and hold the type of youngster that needed Rodney most.

This atmosphere started at the door where, as a matter of policy, there was no mention of membership and no questions were asked. Once inside, this free-and-easy attitude was maintained, and there was no discipline to inhibit the children's activities. In short, they were allowed every opportunity to let off steam. The reason behind this initial laxness was the shrewd suspicion that unless they were given their heads the children might refuse to come, and thus cut themselves off from all that Rodney was trying to do for them.

Naturally, this produced difficulties. Night after night, there were those who went too far. Fights broke out, helpers were beaten up, furniture was wrecked and the police had to be called in.

Gradually, however, things settled down, and with the introduction of indoor football, boxing and wrestling, and bridging the gap between pure recreation and constructive activity, the 'dabbling classes', Rodney entered upon a reign of comparative peace.

These 'dabbling classes' have proved very successful and through them children have been led to interest of a more permanent nature in some 42 different activities, from art and drama to woodwork and beauty culture.

★ ★ ★ ★

Its teething troubles are now over, and in its latest home in Myrtle Street, to which the centre moved in 1953, though animal spirits run high, real trouble has become extremely rare.

Upstairs, in a 14-foot boxing-ring, I watched two pocket-sized and paper-weight Carneras, wearing gloves almost as big as themselves, hammer out their energies harmlessly under the supervision of a trained instructor.

Next door a group of youngsters were practising head rolls and hand stands over a vaulting-horse, while a young man in a wine-coloured P.T. suit, who works during the day as a foreman in a tobacco warehouse, made sure that they did themselves no damage.

Now 9 o'clock – closing time – was fast approaching, and as I descended to the canteen, gingerly negotiating a staircase down which two bellowing urchins were sliding on a large wooden toboggan, I got a wonderful bird's-eye view of the big hall.

I saw the youngsters playing somewhat unconventional billiards, lying across the tables for tricky long shots; watched them dance like dervishes in pursuit of table-tennis balls, and saw the long queue for a last tea and a bun forming at the nothing-over-twopence canteen.

There was just time to peep into one of the class-rooms where I found half a dozen small boys repairing their own shoes under the expert guidance of a cobbler.

This cobbler is just one of sixty big-hearted workers, most of them voluntary, who every week give up precious leisure hours to a work of charity which is none the less praiseworthy because it is enacted upon a small canvas.

It is to these Good Samaritans, every bit as much as to Stella Baker and her staff, that Rodney owes its outstanding success, and as I stepped out into the night street which had once been the children's only playground I felt that Liverpool can be really proud of the work that is being done in an old gymnasium in Myrtle Street for its littlest citizens.

7. WILLINGLY TO SCHOOL

For thousands of Merseyside youngsters, ambition's highway runs through a black smoke-stained building in Mount Street.

During the day this building is the Liverpool Institute, but at night, when the playground is deserted, its class-rooms are filled with a strange company of pupils who have little in common with their diurnal tenantry, except a strong determination to learn.

Round about the time when the majority of young folk, released from shops, offices and a hundred other ways of earning their fifteen or sixteen hours of daily freedom, dispersed merrily for home and an evening of dancing, cinema, television or what have you, a thin column of earnest young figures, mostly carrying small attaché-cases or brief-cases, wound its purposeful way up the symbolically steep hill to the 118-year-old Institute which crowns it. I was among, but, to my shame, not *of* them, and shortly after 5.30 I found myself in a great basement canteen where, sitting on bare forms before scrubbed wood tables in an atmosphere vaguely reminiscent of an O.R.'s mess in the army, a conflux of young men and women ate Welsh rarebit and buns and sipped mugs of steaming tea to put them on until they got home for supper.

I chatted with several of the students. A pretty 18-year-old girl in an orange coat told me, between mouthfuls of poached egg, that she comes once a week for tuition to Mount Street. During the day she works in a city office, but she has set her heart on becoming a radiographer and her maths are not quite up to the required standard. A sergeant in the R.A.M.C. is doing an intensive course in physics in order to qualify as a laboratory technician. A pale young man in glasses is assiduously preparing himself for the examination which will make the transition from the temporary to the established staff of the Civil Service possible for him.

At 6.14 precisely the imperative summons of a loud electric bell sent everyone hustling to his or her class-room. The chatter ceased; the building was suddenly filled with the noise of a great many pairs of feet tramping its uncarpeted stairs and floors, and then . . . silence, in which the occasional sound of a lecturer's muffled voice echoed almost uncannily. It was hard to believe that there were perhaps 250 people in that hushed place.

Guiltily, feeling myself an indolent truant, I tiptoed along sepulchrous stone corridors in company with Mr. L. B. C. Howard, the Principal and, peeping through quietly-opened doors, saw whole roomfuls of cheery Smilesian self-help. Young heads were dutifully bent over dry-as-dust textbooks, teachers drew careful and (to me) incomprehensible chalk signs on blackboards, and outside, another world it seemed, the city shook itself and began to prepare for a night of gaiety.

Make no mistake, it takes courage – great courage – to discipline yourself to come to this place after a hard day's work. These tousle-headed young men who sit at cramping desks designed for their younger brothers are not unnatural creatures who would rather be doing this than playing a game of snooker or having one at the local. These attractive young women are not soulless bluestockings who infinitely prefer an evening's construing of Latin verbs to the delights of circling the dance floor in *his* arms. There is nothing to distinguish them in any way from any of the other young folk who are doing just those things. Nothing, that is, except ambition and the promptings of a self-awareness which whispers that unless you are one of the lucky ones, cosseted, schooled and sent to university by comfortably-situated parents, the only way to success is "To scorn delights, and live laborious days" – or rather nights.

★ ★ ★ ★

At 7.45 the bell will ring again and there will be a fifteen-minute break for coffee and a brief pulling-together of tired wits. Then it is back to the desk, and another hour and a half's wrestle with Euclid, the mind-twisting mysteries of algebra or the infinite complexities of the English language.

By 9.30 another night of work is over and, weary-eyed, the scholars straggle forth, their heads a little heavier with the burden of their hard-won knowledge.

And so it will go on, night after night, until at length the harvest of a well-merited success is reaped and a whole crop of new business executives and recruits to the professions will bring an experience, all the more valuable because it has been acquired in the hard world of the night-school, into whatsoever sphere their grit and industry have entitled them to ascend.

8. HALF-DAY WITH THE MUSES

Splendid museum weather. A grey sunless afternoon, the half-holiday crowds shuffling towards February nagged by a sharp-edged wind. The first Saturday for fifteen years that it was possible to visit a museum in the heart of Liverpool. And so I went to see what old friends I could remeet and what new wonders had been prepared for me. Up the new concrete stairway, gauche and utilitarian-seeming beside the grand sweep of smoke-black steps that lead now only to a great portico and the waste land, to try my luck in the Horseshoe Gallery.

★ ★ ★ ★

"Natural History. Archaeology. Ethnology. Shipping", proclaims the freshly-painted board outside, and entering the gallery you see immediately before you a glass case in which, dull and wicked, lies a great fragment of the bomb that fired the old temple of the Muses. How, one wonders, to classify that? Ethnology I suppose. Man at his nadir. A step or two away, man at his zenith. Scaling Mount Everest, he is represented by a bearded dummy wearing the actual clothes which shielded Dr. Charles Evans from the wind which blows across the roof of the world as he climbed the craggy pinnacles in the successful expedition of 1953. And in the dummy's hand the ice-axe of Everest's old wooer, the late Frank Smythe. A nice touch that.

Nor is it only the literal ascent of man that is here illustrated. In case after case of glittering, splendid things you can follow the whole artistic evolution of the Lord of Creation. You can trace, too, through the arrows of the scientists' careful labels, the 2,000-million-year-history of mankind's emergence from what the old Victorians called the 'brute creation'.

But it was not, in the main, in academic mood that the questing crowds – 2,792 of them that Saturday – came to the museum. They came, father, mother and the children, to see strange and wonderful things, and they were not disappointed.

I stood beside a little family group that gazed in admiration at some of the treasures that the director of the Liverpool Museum has retrieved from the precincts of the Temple of Aphrodite during his excavations at Kouklia (Old Paphos) in Cyprus – sculptured heads deliberately disfigured by the Persians during the first great struggle between Europe and the East at the end of the sixth century B.C. At one time these limestone heads had evidently been richly coloured, and even now careful examination reveals traces of brilliant pigments still upon them after all these years.

Here, too, were gathered fragments of the ancient arts of Egypt and Greece. A huge mummy-case in which once rested the body of Peteamun, nicknamed Ipy, a negro who, 2,300 years ago, captained the Sacred Barque of Amun, and whose coffin is on that account painted with seahorses; the world-famous ancient Egyptian eye-paint vase (an old friend this) of carved wood fashioned in the shape of a slave carrying a water-jar. A poignant little memorial to the lineage of female pride! Perhaps the greatest treasure of the Greek collection is the Diopet. In Ephesus there was a temple in which there stood a great statue of Artemis, and in a shrine which surmounted the crown on the head of this statue was kept the most holy relic of all – a sacred stone called the Diopet. Although, of course, after the lapse of thousands of years its identity cannot be proved, many experts agree that this strange stone object is nothing less than the original Diopet, the sacred stone of Zeus.

But the relic which fascinated me most was an Etruscan cinerary urn made to hold the ashes of a lady named Arui Helesa. She is depicted reclining on the lid and she wears a pair of earrings with pyramidal drops. Within this urn was found a pair of golden earrings identical with those carved upon the lid, undoubtedly the very ones she wore in life. And there they are exhibited beside her funeral cask.

One could linger long in the archaeological and ethnological sections, there is so much to see. Examples of some of man's earliest attempts at writing; one of the actual jars in which the Dead Sea Scrolls were found stored in the caves of Palestine; the magnificent Sassoon collection of Chinese ivories – carvings with such delightful titles as *Seven Worthies of the Bamboo Grove, The Story of Su Ch'in* and *Villa in Paradise*. Then there is a miscellany of more up-to-date ethnological pieces. The prismatic spyglass of an old seadog which must have mystified and disciplined the sailors under his command, for it enabled its owner to see what was happening behind his back; one or two sentimental trifles like the tiny red slippers which once encased the baby feet of King Edward VII, a selection of Queen Alexandra's dresses and some dry and withered sprays of orange-blossom which adorned the wedding-dress of Queen Mary on July 6th, 1893. A pretty puzzle is provided by a small brown ball in one of the glass cases. "What," asked an official, "do you think that is?" I just couldn't begin to guess. It turned out to be a ball of tea-leaves. Such balls are used as money in Tibet, Mongolia and China.

★ ★ ★ ★

It is at the very end of the Horseshoe Gallery that art and nature meet. Man stripped of all his raiments and pretensions, stripped as it were of the buff, a couple of hundred snow-white bones seated, symbolically, upon a beautifully-upholstered chair. A human skeleton side by side with the physically almost identical skeleton of a gorilla, separated from it spiritually by all those centuries of art and artifice. "Eh, dad, what smashing teeth," opines an awe-struck schoolboy. They were lovely indeed. "Wherever did you get such a magnificent specimen?" I asked and seemed to catch an uneasy echo of burke in the official reply, "The history of such acquisitions is always suffocated!"

★ ★ ★ ★

And then I am in Wonderland, surrounded by beautiful birds, stuffed and mounted with such artistry as I have never before seen. These surely are not dead but living things. The graceful coot crying to the night against a cunningly contrived background of infinity and the blood of a dying sun. Tiny fluffy balls of new-born birds backed by the fathomless blue of a morning sky. A breathtaking group of waders captured, eternally immobile, in the mobile-seeming moment, and standing upon a solid ground of real mud painstakingly transported here from Parkgate. Even snakes, which I am told are over a hundred years old and have been rescued from the cramped sarcophagi of jars of spirit, have, after a skilful and entirely new technique of treatment at the hands of Mr. Reginald Wagstaffe (Keeper of the Department of Vertebrate Zoology), the very aspect of life.

It is a Wonderland in which time indeed diminishes, for in the beautifully-arranged botanical section actual specimens of great ferns which lived all of 250 million years ago glow green with life beneath the resuscitating rays of an ultra-violet lamp.

The microscopic secrets of a Cheshire pond; lovely fronds of seaweed splayed upon illuminated glass; a richly-coloured diorama of the autumn woodland and its fungi; even the rarely-seen leaves of the coca-plant which yields cocaine (imported only with the greatest difficulty); they are all here.

And finally, after dallying over cases containing crabs that climb trees and feast on coconuts, molluscs whose bite can mean death, tarantulas whose bite, contrary to popular belief, is harmless, moths with a tip-to-tip wing span of nearly a foot, and insects protectively formed and coloured so that they are practically indistinguishable from leaves, I came upon a tiny worm-like creature from South Africa. It is unique, supplying the 'missing line' between the worms and the insects. It spends most of its days asleep beneath logs and stones and is seldom seen. But at night it becomes alert and adventurous. I doubt if any of the other 2,791 visitors even noticed it, but I read its little label with a curious sense of familiarity . . . its name is PERIPATUS.

9 READERS' RETREAT

Domed, like the round skull of an intellectual, looms the rotund bulk of the Picton Reference Library – Liverpool's Temple of Literature.

Outside, on this bitter February day, a powder of snow sets a white wig on its bald black brow. Inside, a centrally-heated silence in which the whisperings of resentfully-parting pages raise a sibilance of echoes. It is as if, high in the Pantheonic dome, the Muses conspire upon which bent head they will bestow wisdom.

But for all its silence this is a battleground; the restless front of learning. And, bearing their battle-scars of lined brows and red myopic eyes, the warriors sit in radiating rows of desks, ordered or disordered as their minds, the bent heads of senility and the challenging heads of youth.

Here is Hope: a young girl, bright, pert and clear-eyed, screwing a truant curl about her finger as she wrestles with a stout treatise on mathematics. There, next to her, is Resignation: an old white-beared man in a velvet skull-cap, covering page after page with a spider scrawl of notes culled from a big black leather volume.

And so it has been ever since 1879 when this great library, built out of public funds and named after Sir James Allanson Picton, the Liverpool historian and at that time chairman of the Library, Museum and Arts Committee, first opened its doors.

Across the years the young have sought and found knowledge in this vast book-lined rotunda. Age has here consolidated experience. And here, too, some have suffered the death of youth and the strangulation of belief. What a motley collection of hatibués the place has gathered to itself. They come and go like spectres:

"Cranks, hacks, poverty-stricken scholars,
In pince-nez, period hats or romantic beards
And cherishing their hobby or their doom
Some are too much alive and some are asleep
Hanging like bats in a world of inverted values,
Folded up in themselves in a world which is safe and silent."

Like Louis MacNeice's stooping haunted readers in the British Museum Reading Room.

★ ★ ★ ★

At one time or another some quest drives all of us to the quiet alcoves of the Picton – to turn yellowing archives in the local history section, to pin an elusive fact, to plant a genealogical tree, to uproot an old mystery. Here are the serried ranks of local newspapers, dating from 1756: the rows of Liverpool directories, beginning at the year 1766. Upon miles of shelves, from floor to ceiling, and in thousands of tea-chests, deep from sight in hidden storerooms, are crammed more than a million items – books and pamphlets, maps and manuscripts. The oldest fragment of writing is a scrap of Liverpool's original Charter. Dated 1207, it is kept in a small glass-topped box. And in a fireproof safe is the Picton's most ancient printed book, a copy of Petrarch's "Sonnets," printed in Venice in 1407, which once graced the shelves of William Roscoe. The most valuable work in the library is Audubon's "Birds of America". It is worth more than £12,000. It has also the distinction of being the largest book in the Picton, each of its four volumes measuring fully three feet in height and nearly as much in width. Requiring two men to lift it comfortably, it is well-styled bibliographically a double elephant folio! Side by side with this mammoth, I was shown the smallest book in the collection, a minute copy of the Koran scarcely larger than a postage-stamp. Bound in red, tooled with golden oriental designs, it nestles in a tiny chased silver case in the lid of which is inset a very necessary magnifying glass.

★ ★ ★ ★

The care and conservation of this huge and variegated collection of books is only one part of the duties of the staff. They must also be ever ready to help and guide the serious inquirer. Some of the inquiries are, to say the least, unusual. What is the origin of a chemist's coloured bottles? Which part of the peacock was eaten in Roman times? What was the etiquette and costume of the Portuguese court in Brazil between 1808 and 1830? A schoolgirl wants advice on making wigs for dolls. A lady would like to know the correct time for cutting capers. This last request caused some perplexity until it was suddenly realised that she was referring to the plants in the garden.

And somehow or other all these awkward questions are answered, though sometimes, when the encyclopaedias and other learned tomes have failed to yield a solitary clue, the information turns up on the back of one of the cigarette-cards, a magnificent collection of which forms a cartophilist's corner of paradise in the gallery of a small back room.

★ ★ ★ ★

And so, day in day out (Sunday excepted), the reading and the searching go ceaselessly on from 9 a.m. to 9 p.m., when the gong shatters the day-long silence and sends the last lingering reader flitting out between the dusky pillars. Out from the steam-heated security of his bookish hideaway, past the pallid moon-washed statues into the frosty reality of the neon-hung night.

10 OLYMPIAN GHOSTS

The lights were low, the music sweet, and the girls in their pretty coloured frocks drifted gracefully through the sea of dusk like so many bright flowers floating upon the surface of some darkling pool.

Alone, I sat in what had once been the grand circle of the old Olympia Theatre and watched the couples waltz around the floor of the dance-hall which it has become. Beneath the bare proscenium and past the empty boxes, the whisper of their feet echoing to the ornate ceiling.

The place was crowded and very gay, but for all that, I found in it much of that strange melancholy atmosphere which always clings about old buildings which have once been theatres; the feeling that sad-eyed ghosts are perpetually waiting in the wings for the cue that never comes.

And what ghosts must linger beyond the limes in the old Olympia! The names of those who played its boards read like a history of the British theatre. Seymour Hicks as Scrooge; Louie Freear in *The Little Marchioness* – an adaptation of Dickens's *Old Curiosity Shop;* Ethel Levey in *Watch Your Step;* Sir Henry Irving's Son, Lawrence, in *The Ballad-Monger* and the great and glamorous Gaby Deslys who, so it is said, did most successfully mulct Manuel of Portugal. Here, too, hover the lighter shades of such immortal troupers as Gus Ellen, Mark Sheridan, George Formby senior, Albert Chevalier and Wilkie Bard.

★ ★ ★ ★

And now they are all gone; the curtain has fallen for the last time; the call-boy's voice is stilled and the youth of Liverpool rock 'n' roll where once Pavlova – the incomparable Swan – twirled and pirouetted like a fragment of wind-tossed thistle-down.

This was the theatre in which, one wild wet night during the Kaiser's war, that felicitous diarist, the late Ian Mackay, then a private in the R.A.M.C., climbed happily up into the gods to hear Dainty Daisy Dormer tunefully tell him that she wouldn't leave her little wooden hut for him. Here it was that Liverpool first heard Wagner's cycle, *The Ring,* performed by the Quinlan Opera Company, and here the slightly cloying music of Puccini's *Girl of the Golden West* first sounded on grey north-western air.

Nor was it only legitimate theatre and the fluffier fare of the music-hall that flourished at the old Olympia. Every so often the circus would come to town, the orchestra pit and the first dozen or so rows of the stalls would be cleared and a huge sawdust ring erected. You can still see the place where they used to keep the elephants. It is now being made into a restaurant, artfully contrived with plastic and plaster to look like the baronial hall of a mediaeval castle.

★ ★ ★ ★

Then there were the famous water spectacles, when a gigantic circular water-tank took the place of the circus-ring. I found it derelict in the basement, rusted and grime and as dry as a bone.

It was in this very tank that the notorious Louis de Rougemont (according to some the greatest mountebank since Munchausen), whose impossible adventures were retailed to a gasping audience of our grandparents in the monthly pages of *The Wide World Magazine,* actually rode, within living memory, on the back of a turtle. It was in this tank, too, that Ethel Haydon, tied to a stake by the villain in *The Sands of Dee,* was very nearly drowned when the waters were accidentally allowed to rise considerably higher than the stage directions specified.

★ ★ ★ ★

Back upstairs, a crooner with one of those pseudo-American accents which are all the go nowadays had begun to sing. "Happy, happy baby" he intoned into the microphone (how the great stars of yesterday would have scorned to use a microphone) over and over again, and I could not help thinking that Uncle Sam has won as complete and bloodless a victory here in this ancient stronghold of the English stage as he appears to have achieved at the London Palladium. "I know my happy baby loves her guy"! I wonder what the old-timers would think of *those* lovely lyrics.? Not very much, I fear. But of one thing I am certain. They might not understand the changes which time has brought, but they, who devoted their lives to giving pleasure, would see gladly that in its new life their beloved theatre is filled still with happy young people.

11 AN OLD MASTER

It is not every day that you stumble upon a priceless 'Old Master', but this week I have done just that. I hasten to say that I claim no credit for this discovery of mine, for it was in fact a splendid example of that whimsical combination of circumstances for which Horace Walpole coined the word 'serendipity', which he defined as "the making of discoveries, by accident and sagacity, of things you were not in quest of."

This is how it came about.

For some considerable time now I have been engaged in writing the life of that famous Liverpool poet of the nineties, Richard Le Gallienne, and in the course of my researches I learned that Le Gallienne's parents had been married, nearly a hundred years ago, at St. Jude's Church in Hardwick Street. Naturally, this information sent me hotfoot to St. Jude's in order to examine the old registers in the vestry, and while there I decided to have a peep at the interior of the church itself. It proved, as I had expected, a pleasing early nineteeth-century church, commodious and clean of line, though not, perhaps, architecturally distinguished, but what I had not been prepared for was the magnificent picture which hung above the high-altar.

The picture was large, some 8 by 5½ feet, set in a broad gilt frame, and represented Christ hanging upon His cross. With its striking arrangement of light and shade, it was absolutely compelling. Its presence irradiated the entire church and became the focal point of the whole interior. Indeed, so impressed by it was I, that I felt convinced that it was not ordinary painting and decided there and then to go and see the vicar and ask him what he knew of its history.

The Reverend Arthur J. Petford received me most cordially in the cosy study of his Erskine Street vicarage. "So you have discovered our picture," he said. "You are quite right, it is no ordinary painting. We have reason to believe that it is a genuine Zurbarán and worth a considerable sum of money."

Francisco de Zurbarán (1598-1644) was a Spanish painter of considerable renown. A native of Fuente de Cantos, he came of a family of peasants, but his artistic interests and exceptional talent soon took him to Seville. There in the year 1625, he was commissioned to paint an altarpiece for the cathedral, and in 1650 was appointed one of the official artists to King Philip IV, in consequence of which he spent the remainder of his life in Madrid.

"But how on earth does a picture by a Spanish master come to be hanging in the obscure little Liverpool church of St. Jude?" I asked. The vicar told me all he knew of its history. It was in 1906 that the then vicar of St. Jude's, Canon Algernon Augustus Markham (later Bishop of Grantham), saw the painting, unframed, in a picture shop on the north side of St. Luke's Church, Berry Street. He made inquiries concerning it of the dealer and found that by a curious coincidence it had belonged to a friend of his, Mr. Richard Willis of Halsnead. Willis's grandfather had bought it in Paris in the 'fifties, and he had stored it in London after first insuring it for £1,000. When he died, his successor kept the picture in storage but dropped the insurance. Many years later it descended to Richard Willis who had it sent down to Halsnead, but considering the subject unsuitable for his drawing-room, he first decided to present it to the Roman Catholic chapel at Rainhill, but later changed his mind and sent it to Liverpool to be sold for what it would fetch. The picture dealer warned Mr. Willis that that would not be much and, though he informed Canon Markham that he half suspected that it was a Spagnoletto, he was content to sell it to him for a very small sum, and the Canon, after having it cleaned and framed, hung it, not without trepidation because of its papistic tone, over the main altar of his church. How it originally came into the hands of Willis's grandfather is a matter concerning which, in the absence of any definite evidence, it is only possible to speculate. The discovery of Zurbarán beyond the Pyrenees dates back to the Napoleonic Wars, at which time the French admired his paintings so intensely that they sacked them by the dozen from the churches of Seville. It may well be that this painting was one of those looted by Napoleon and brought by him to Paris. Again, Louis Philippe had a great collection of Spanish paintings, acquired during the secularization of the Spanish monasteries in 1835, which was broken up and sold in 1853.

Canon Markham afterwards wrote: "I thought it would be useful and interesting to hear what the art authorities of the city had to say about it . . . so I made my way to the curator and explained there was a reputed 'Old Master' within ten minutes walk in St. Jude's Church. Would he be so kind as to look at it? The curator turned in his writing-table chair, looked at me and said, 'Do you think I've nothing better to do than go and look at other people's pictures?' But somebody turned up and declared that he knew of the picture and that it was by Zurbarán."

"There had been a recent and striking confirmation of that diagnosis," said Mr. Petford, "for when, a while back, I sent the picture to be cleaned, I received a letter from the firm of restorers asking me if I knew that what I had sent them was a genuine Zurbarán."

★ ★ ★ ★

Having heard all this, I rushed down to the Art Library to see the librarian, Mr. Keith Andrews. To my surprise – and disappointment – he knew all about the picture. "Last November," he told me, "I happened to pick up a parish magazine in my dentist's waiting-room and read in it that there was a fine oil-painting in St. Jude's Church. A day or two later I went to see it. I was very impressed by it and thought at first that it was a Ribera (José de Ribera was a Spanish painter of the same period as Zurbarán, and it was he who was nicknamed 'Spagnoletto' by the Italians). On closer examination, however, I was convinced that it was a Zurbarán." Mr. Andrews told his colleague, Mr. Hugh Scrutton, director of the Walker Art Gallery, of his discovery and he, too, went to have a look at it. "In my opinion the painting may well be a genuine Zurbarán," Mr. Scrutton told me.

★ ★ ★ ★

Let those who affirm that there is no romance to be found in present-day Liverpool read this as a cautionary tale, for it is indeed fascinating to think that for half a century an 'Old Master', worth perhaps £10,000, has hung, dusty and unrecognised, in a remote Victorian church in the centre of our city. Serendipidists everywhere, take heart!

12 AFTER THE DUSTCART . . .

There is a time-honoured saying, "After the Lord Mayor's Show comes the dustcart" and, in Liverpool at any rate, that observation has something rather firmer than a philosophic basis, for it is to the corporation cleansing-yard that you must go if you wish to take a closer look at the magnificent Lord Mayor's carriage, normally glimpsed only from afar as it bowls colourfully along on state occasions.

So it was that I, together with two American friends, hot on the trail of what they called 'British tradition,' made overtures to Mr. Richard Wilson, the city cleansing-superintendent, who, under city engineer Mr. H. T. Hough, has charge of the dustcarts and the mayoral cars and carriages, to see the 136-year-old state coach. "Certainly," he said, and we followed a lumbering dustcart into the Smithdown Lane cleansing-yard, turned sharp right and there, snug in an electrically heated garage, stood the Lord Mayor's show piece.

"Gee!" said 23-year-old Donald Hickinbotham from Stockton, California, "I seen some of the old prairie-schooners (covered wagons) back home, but this sure is something." And lolling back on the claret-coloured upholstery, his friend, Roger Wethey, who hails from Watsonville, California, closed his eyes and added, "This sure is comfort."

How right they were. Built in 1820 by Gorst & Co., carriage makers of Great Charlotte Street, Liverpool's state coach certainly is exquisite. You have only to clamber up its folding, carpeted steps into it to feel that you really *are* a Lord Mayor. All its parts are hand-made, and each one of them, from the door-handles to the perfectly-fitting blinds, functions with a smooth efficiency which bespeaks the highest craftmanship. The candle lamps gleam, the springs yield noiselessly and the coat of arms, handpainted on the side by W. H. Starkey, a local heraldic artist, about 1907, still has about it an unblemished freshness which makes it difficult to realise that its colours dried fifty years ago. Only the upholstery is new. That was renovated two years ago for the first time in more than a century and a quarter.

★ ★ ★ ★

In a nearby stable the six horses who take it in turn to draw, two by two, Liverpool's First Citizen through the streets, were having their evening meal. These horses come from Holland and are specially selected for the job. They are all beautiful animals and stand seventeen hands high – an essential qualification this – and their stud names are Yorke, Yeoman, Yarrow, Walnut, Wanderer and Wellington, though they are known affectionately, if less grandly, as Bobby, Dick, Prince, Teddy, Laddie and Porky. Apparently it is a convention of the stable never to address a horse by its stud name.

The training of these horses is all done at Smithdown Lane. They begin by going round and round the cobbled yard on a long rein. After that they learn their manners drawing a light lorry round the yard. Next they are put between the shafts of a large green brake, and finally they go out in the brake to get used to road work. At the end of 4-6 weeks they are ready for their important state work. I noticed a small wireless on one of the window-ledges in the stable. "Are the horses musical?" I asked. "They've got to be," replied Mr. Wilson. "We have this radio here and every time there is a brass band concert we put it on full blast. The horses get used to it and are not upset when they encounter loud ceremonial music in the course of their work." Suddenly there was a sharp burst of what sounded like machine-gun fire. I almost leapt into the air. The horses went on unconcernedly munching. A groom stood in the doorway. He had one of those villainous wooden rattles that one sees – and hears – at football matches in his hand. "We use that to accustom them to sudden unexpected noises," laughed Mr. Wilson, 'otherwise they might shy like you did and cause a lot of damage."

★ ★ ★ ★

In the harness-room we were introduced to Liverpool's only working coachman, 42-year-old Walter Holden. In that shining place where the walls glistened with polished leather and mirror-bright brass and the very air seemed edged with elbow-grease, Mr. Holden told us how he started as a stable-boy at the age of sixteen. When we met him Mr. Holden was – except for a vividly-checked waistcoat – dressed soberly enough, but when he is on the box he is a startingly resplendent figure. His summer uniform, proudly displayed to us in the livery room, consists of a plum-coloured, liberally-braided, velvet body-coat, a brilliant waistcoat with glinting gold buttons, black-and-gold breeches, white silk stockings and shiny black buckle-shoes. In winter he wears a huge frilled greatcoat, just like those the coachmen wear on Christmas cards. On state occasions he dons a black-and-gold tricorn and a grey wig. ("His work is so worrying he goes grey every time he turns out," quipped Mr. Wilson). I was allowed to try the wig and tricorn on. I thought it looked rather impressive. "You look like the man on the Quaker oats packet," said Mr. Wilson. I removed them hurriedly. In full regalia Mr. Holden appears so different that when she first saw him his own wife failed to recognise him, and he still tells with glee of how a former Lord Mayor once came up and asked him where he could find the old grey-headed man who had driven him.

"Say, how long does it take you to turn out with all this stuff in an emergency?" asked one of the Americans doubtfully.

“We can be on the road inside thirty minutes,” was the reply.

“My! That’s certainly moving,” said the astounded visitor, “and they say we’re fast over there.”

“We’ll have to tell the mayor of San Francisco he’s behind the times when we get back, I guess,” chimed in his companion. “He’s only got a car.”

And two very impressed young Americans went off to pack their bags and tell the folks ‘back home’ of the wonders they had encountered in a Liverpool ‘muck-yard.’

13 THE PIPES OF PAN AND THE SERPENT

I had always thought of the pipes of Pan as green, but they weren't. Neither were they cut from river reeds, but baked in clay 2,000 years ago, buried for countless springs in the sands of Lima and, after being excavated in 1909, brought to Liverpool to become one of the star exhibits in the Rushworth and Dreaper collection of antique musical instruments.

Let me confess, as I made my way upstairs to the ghostly grey room which houses a vast and silent orchestra, I had secret hopes that I might perhaps encounter Signor Ubaldo Ubaldi: or rather, *part* of Signor Ubaldi, for when that admirable Italian music lover laid his clarinet and quitted his native Bologna for somewhere where the harp is held supreme, he left a sum of lire equivalent to £12 and the express instruction that his bones should be made into clarinet mouthpieces!

Instead, I met a genial and kindly curator who made no bones about his love of the history of music and gently guided my ignorant steps from the syrinx (the aforesaid Pan-pipes of the Chimu dynasty) via the lyre, cor anglais and flageolet, to the latest note in music, a startingly white and stream-lined electronic organ.

"Have you ever seen a serpent?" he asked suddenly. I muttered something about the zoo which, with winning tact, he pretended not to hear as he led me towards a small mahogany table upon which lay a black leathery twist of cornet. It was the ancient serpent. The instrument is apparently obsolete now, but once upon a time it was a prime ecclesiastical favourite and sent many a heavenly blast of plainsong soaring to the steeple.

★ ★ ★ ★

We had a bit of trouble over the hurdy-gurdy, too.

I had pointed ecstatically to an exceptionally fine specimen of one of those bright-painted instruments which in the long-ago you used to see being trundled through the yellow streets by some sweating Italian street-musician.

"It is NOT a hurdy-gurdy," said the curator with some acerbity, "*That* is a hurdy-gurdy," he indicated a small instrument in one of the glass cases. It struck me as looking rather like a sawn-off mandoline and it had a little handle attached to a circular bow. It was very beautiful and, I gathered, somewhat rare.

"I'm sorry," I said hastily, "I meant barrel-organ."

That was definitely the wrong thing to say.

"It is NOT a barrel-organ: *that* is a barrel-organ."

I stood blushing in the shade of a monstrous wooden cabinet amply endowed with organ pipes.

"The barrel-organ is a mechanical organ which was extensively employed at the beginning of the 19th century in churches where there was difficulty in obtaining an organist. The cumbrous, wheeled instrument to which the monkey used to 'dance' was a street-piano."

After that I decided upon the wisdom of silence. I absolutely refused to be drawn concerning the sheng (a Chinese portable organ of great antiquity which was the precursor of the reed-organ) or the fagotto (another name for the bassoon which stems from its fancied resemblance to a bundle of sticks) but could not refrain from commenting upon the freakish bottle-organ.

The specimen which I was shown was built in 1798 and was actually used for many years in a church in Heligoland. The instrument is a unique combination of piano and organ and the fascinating thing about it is that the organ note is produced by blowing air across the mouths of a series of bottles which are clearly visible lying in dusty graduated rows inside the body of the instrument.

The gulf between organs and pianos thus effectively bridged, we turned to elegant spinets, Venetian virginals, harpsichords and clavichords – this latter, by the way, the only true forerunner of the modern piano. I was shown a miniature piano no more than a foot long and exquisitely matched by a tiny kit violin. The kit or dancing-master's violin was, as its name implies, much in demand for dancing-teachers who would carry it in their pockets and scrape a lively accompaniment upon it in the days before the piano had become the ubiquitous music-maker of the drawing room. I saw, too, but did not admire, a large and ugly upright piano which had come from Speke Hall and was hideously encrusted with porcelain plates of flowers.

★ ★ ★ ★

And then, at last, we came to the prize piece of the whole collection, a grand-pianoforte which, more than a hundred years ago, stood in the music-room of Oberglogau Castle in Saxony, and upon which, during his visits to Count von Oppersdorf, the great Beethoven himself would frequently play.

"Would you care to hear it?" asked the curator, and he sat down and, very gently, ran his fingers along the keys. After a minute or two he slid into a Beethoven study and as I stood listening to that music played on that piano moving to a crescendo, I forgot the man at the keyboard. Suddenly I had a picture of another in his place . . . a great leonine head bent as though listening. But *he* could never have done that, for those strong squat hands crashing derisive chords in the faces of the Gods belonged to a man who, though his genius commanded the ear of the world, was himself stone-deaf.

14 JAZZ WAVES OF THE MERSEYSIPPI

At 8 o'clock every Sunday evening 400 or so 'cats' pay their eager 3s. to sit in the back room of Liverpool's Temple Restaurant and listen to a fishmonger, a bus conductor, a company director, a gentleman of leisure and four clerks spend their spare time bringing the tortured music of the Deep South to the heart of the Sunday-night city, and the other Sunday I decided that I would join them.

Upstairs on the bus that bore me through the treetops of bosky Prince's Boulevard, past dark Victorian churches, where solemn groups stood, handshaking, in the yellow-lit frames of porches, sitting in on a jazz session suddenly struck me as a queer way of passing a Sunday night, but as I walked up the murky little passageway which led to the jazz club, the distant throb and beat of drums, the whining of an anguished clarinet and the blare and burst of brass drove all other thoughts from my head.

A door opened: a blast of hot music caught me by the ears, and there I was in a room bathed in orange light, pillared and arched with a bastard Moorish-Spanish décor and pierced with glassless, plywood windows through which one glimpsed painted hills clambered by those glistening white and red-tiled houses that one remembers stark in the hard sunlight that bakes the olive hills about Tangier.

The Merseysippi band was 'giving' with a vengeance.

"What are they playing?" I shouted above the din.

" 'The Saints Go Marching In,' " replied a young man in a violent red shirt. "It's a hymn tune – hotted up, of course." I'll say it was hotted up. It sounded more like a flame-licked lament from hell than an overture to heaven. Still, I felt that it was a happy tribute to the fact that it was Sunday. And later, when I ventured to interrupt the swooning delight of a pretty girl in a sweater that looked exactly as though she had rolled up a zebra crossing and wrapped it tightly about her bosom, with a request for the title of a particularly rumbustious piece which was shattering my eardrums, I was tersely informed that it was a New Orleans funeral march. "Hotted up, of course," I said weakly and relapsed into silence.

Looking around the room I decided that I must try to find out just what it was that brought 400 young people out on a miserable wet night, not to dance, but just to sit quietly on rows of chairs, rapt and serious, differing from the average Philharmonic audience only in that their bodies swayed and rocked, their feet tapped, and their fingers drummed, and that they clapped their hands in time with the music, occasionally screamed and had a rather glazed look in their eyes.

In an interval of sweet silence I spoke to 20-year-old Adrienne Ferst. She works behind a post-office counter all week. Comes here every Sunday. She looked at me as though I were a little mad when I asked her why she came. "Why? Because the music sends me," she said, and tossed back a glass of tomato juice like a veteran. "Have you heard 'Nineteen-Nineteen'? she queried. I admitted that I hadn't. "You wait till you do then; it'll drive you crazy." I felt sure she was quite right. I spoke to half a dozen other addicts – young doctors, lawyers and civil servants among them. None of them could explain precisely what 'being sent' was, but they all assured me that they were nevertheless 'sent' by the music. 20-year-old Rob Williams, a surveyor, gave me the most coherent explanation: "The rhythm and beat create an atmosphere of excitement."

A voice through the microphone announced, "And now, in memory of a gentleman who died of natural causes, 'My Bucket's Got a Hole In it'." This was greeted with howls of laughter. The joke was too subtle for me. After hearing the piece, however, I am not disposed to disagree that the bucket *had* a hole in it, moreoever I am convinced that it was also filled with pebbles. Then they played "Snake Rag." I thought it was "Snake *Rack*." It should have been.

But it was "Mack the Knife" that sent them further than anything else. The fishmonger devoted himself to scales with a virtuosity which, if equalled in his shop, should put him at the top of his trade. The bus conductor conducted with his foot like a man bitten by a tarantula. While the trombone slid to a height that assaulted the ear with the high-frequency agony of an ice-cream on the exposed nerve of a tooth. The lyric – to me quite unintelligible – was sung by a young man so thin that he must surely have been 'The Knife' himself, and he was succeeded, vocally, by another young man so fat that I felt tradition demand his being christened 'Jelly Roll.'

By 10.30, when the charivari came to an end, not with a whimper but an outsize bang on the drum, I was completely bewildered.

Perhaps, with patience, I can learn to like such music. It may be that I have been missing something in life all these years. I must buy a few records – or rather, 'discs' I believe they are called nowadays – and play them over and over again on my ancient, horned phonograph. Or perhaps I am already too old to learn. This is after all the music of the young – the folk music of the Atom Age – and a man who is even now beginning to find that policemen look incredibly young is, I am told, exhibiting the first disquieting symptoms of advancing senility.

Anyway, I may as well confess it, the Merseysippi music did not send me – except in search of an all-night chemist who could give me something for a headache.

15 THE INSIDE STORY OF LIVERPOOL'S BIG BEN

Mercifully there was a lift: I had dreaded the prospect of those 483 steps.

"This way," said Mr. Corden and without another word he led me straight into the mechanical heart of England's biggest clock.

Mr. James Corden, by the way, is the Engineer at the Liver Buildings and he is also the Keeper of the Clock – the man who is responsible for Liverpool's time.

The Western Clock-Chamber into which I followed him is a large, whitewashed apartment which somehow reminded me of an outsize pigeon-loft. As soon as the little door which leads into it had been unlocked, I became aware of a curious click-clacking noise. It sounded for all the world as if a great flock of giant pigeons was interminably pecking at a wooden floor.

"That's caused by the escapement-wheels," explained Mr. Corden, wiping his hands upon the piece of cotton-waste which engineers always carry and which seems to be as beloved a professional symbol as a doctor's stethoscope. I said, "Oh, yes," and tried to look as if such horological technicalities were not utterly beyond me.

Feeling extraordinarily dwarfed, I stood in the centre of the Clock-Chamber, on three sides of which the vast, opalescent dials of Great George – that is the Liver clock's name – soared ceilingwards. The fourth clock-face reigns in splendid isolation in the Eastern tower. Seen in close-up, the dials are positively overpowering. Each measuring 25 feet in diameter, they beat London's Big Ben by a full 2½ feet. How many, one wonders, of the crowds who queue nightly within the shadow of these Gargantuan timepieces realise that the bus for which they are patiently waiting is a mere matter of twelve inches longer than the edge to edge stretch of one of those bland clock-faces? Even stranger, is the fact that once, in the long-ago, before Great George had been hoisted to his turret top, he did service as a luncheon-table. It was to mark the achievement of Messrs. Gents, in whose Leicester workshops the remarkable piece of clockwork had been brought to life, that some forty leading lights sat themselves primly about the perimeter of one of those dials to enjoy a suitably festive luncheon-party.

Across these gigantic surfaces creep 14-foot minute-hands, unendingly circling the 48 minute-marks, each of which is separated from its neighbour by a distance of 14 inches.

"What kind of numerals are used to show the hours?" asked the engineer suddenly.

"Roman," I replied without hesitation.

"Everyone says that," smiled Corden. "As a matter of fact the hour-marks are not numerals at all. They are just plain black lines each of which is three feet high."

Behind each clock-face is a large circle of white-distempered wall. This is the reflector and is of exactly the same size as the dial which it backs. Between this wall and the dial are hung six sodium lighting-tubes equipped with small sheets of opalescent glass. This arrangement concentrates the light onto the reflector which rediffuses it evenly through the clock-face and produces so good an effect at night that experts regard the Liver clock as one of the best illuminated in the world. At one time the efficiency of the reflectors was briefly menaced by a public who so far misunderstood their purpose as to regard them as a species of monster visitors' books. Many people apparently suffer from a Bill-Stumps-like conviction that it is required of them to leave their mark behind. Such individuals seem to descry in any expanse of bare, white wall an irresistible invitation to scrawl their names upon it. Gradually the signatures mounted, until at last they reached a height of 15 feet from the floor! Many famous names figures among these mural graphiti, but no matter how brightly some of the names may have shone they did not compensate for the overall dimming of the reflectors which their presence produced. Now the reflectors have been redistempered and I read dismay in Mr. Corden's face as he spotted a couple of recent scribblings which had appeared on their virgin whiteness.

After that, we ascended to a narrow, iron-railed gallery which runs around the entire clock-chamber at a height of about 15 feet. Here, in glass cases, is lodged the actual mechanism of the clock. There is a separate works to each clock-face, but these are all controlled by a master-clock which is situated 200 feet below in the main entrance hall of the building. The clock is powered by electricity and runs off batteries which are trickle charged.

It is Mr. Corden's daily task to see that Great George is right. He takes his responsibility very seriously. Every morning at 10 a.m. there is a careful time-check.

"How is it done?" echoed the Keeper of the Clock. "Simply by lifting the telephone and dialing 'TIM.' We check it again at 1 o'clock when the Birkenhead gun goes off."

Sometimes people ring up and complain that the clock is wrong. Every complaint is carefully investigated. One man kept telephoning and insisting that the clock was three minutes slow and added bitterly that for the last few nights he had missed his bus through it. On investigation it transpired that he had been craning his head out of a nearby office window and had been looking at the clock from such an angle that he got an entirely wrong impression of the position of the minute-hand. To get an accurate reading you must view the clock full on. Mr. Corden got his worst-ever fright one day when, looking up, he saw to his horror that all the faces on the Western Tower were showing different times. One dial was ten minutes slow, one fifteen minutes slow and one twenty minutes slow! The explanation lay in the fact that a party of over fifty Dutch children, who had been allowed to visit the clock-chamber, had succumbed to the temptation to lay hands on the pendulums. Such an occurrence underlines the wisdom of the Committee of Management's ruling that all persons obtaining permission to visit the clock must now be accompanied by an official.

Actually, Mr. Corden's proudest boast is that Great George is never more than 7 seconds out, which, all things considered, is a wonderful record. Although it is scarcely possible for Corden to take his work home with him, he does his best to keep an eye on it long after the fingers of his charge have pointed the hour for his day's labours to end. Many a night he leans out from a top window of his home, three miles away in Birkenhead, and takes an affectionate peep at Great George through a telescope, "just to make sure that all is well."

It was a few minutes to five when we left the clock-chamber and made our way up a winding stone stairway to the cupola above Great George. 300 odd feet up, we came out into the strong, fresh wind which always sweeps the roof of Liverpool. Below, the city stretched like a toy town with the silver ribbon of the Mersey unwinding to the horizon. From this point the Great Orme at Llandudno is easily visible and on a clear day you can just see Blackpool Tower. In the centre of the cupola there is a kind of slate-coloured, conical stack from the top of which project eight loud-speakers, carefully protected against the vagaries of the weather by neat plastic covers. These are the veritable mouthpieces of the clock. Although Great George came to Merseyside to mark the Coronation of King George V in 1911, it was not until another Coronation Year, forty-two years later, that this marvellous turret-clock found a voice. Hitherto it has been silent because of the tremendous weight of bells which would have been necessary to give it tongue. Today, however, cumbersome bells are at a discount, their deep-throated chimes can be produced electronically. Below in the clock-chamber, there is a mysterious grey-painted cabinet in which tiny automatic hammers strike slender wires and their tinkling vibrations, amplified hundreds of times, are relayed to the loud-speakers above.

Just then there came a loud, humming, electric sort of sound through the loud-speakers.

"The chimes are warming up," commented Mr. Corden.

Although I was half expecting it, when the first chime thundered out I nearly fell off the roof with fright. In that instant I knew how Theseus must have felt when he heard the bellow of the Minotaur. The impact of the chime was like a brazen artillery firing in one's head; it was deafening, soul-splitting: the entire tower seemed to rock. Surely, I thought, the whole of Liverpool will rush forth in terror. But not a bit of it: no one even looked up. All that happened was that some of the 3,000 people who work daily on the

40,000 square feet of the 17 floors of the towering cliff of masonry which Great George crowns, began to spill out into the streets like a dark column of worker-ants. And I just went on standing there, my ears singing in tune with the great waves of sound which kept ringing out over the cold, wide estuary.

16 THE FABULOUS NATIONAL

Every March, the month of the lion and the lamb, sees Liverpool the brief focal point of the world's eyes. In cars and trains, in ships and aeroplanes, the great sporting world descends upon us: quiet bars hum to the rich brogues of Ireland, the drawling voices of the south and a host of unaccustomed accents. In their thousands they come, the aristocrats and the mountebanks, the race-lovers and the gamblers, and through the grey industrial pattern of our streets is woven a temporary filament of the rainbow. Whispered tips are in abundance. They may be sought in the feathered brilliance of a Monolulu or in the less conspicuous, but often more convincing, horsy shabbiness of a horde of knowledgeable, checked, booted and breeched tipsters. All is bustle and excitement for there is abroad the perennial spirit of the greatest steeplechase in the world.

But if it is upon the course at Aintree that the mounting tide of tension reaches its climax in a noisy, all-submerging wave, its presence is still felt in the lesser currents that surge and eddy through the quieter streets of sedately distant suburbs, where the usually cautious permit themselves the rare indiscretion of their annual "little flutter" upon what seems to them to be their own particular race. And is it not only proper that we should take a pride in our Grand National, for, not only is it a race of noble tradition, but it is the oldest annual steeplechase in the world.

Although the "Sport of Kings," in its classic, flat-racing form, has been in favour since such remote times as the Greek Olympiads of 600 B.C., steeplechasing, or wildgoose chasing, is of much more recent origin.

It all started in Ireland in 1752, when a certain Mr. Edmund Blake accepted a Mr. O'Callaghan's challenge to decide the relative merits of two hunters by means of a cross-country horse-race to be run over the 4¼ miles which separated the church of Buttevant from the spire of St. Leger's church at Doneraile in County Cork. As the St. Leger steeple was visible throughout, the match was facetiously dubbed a "Steeplechase." The idea of making wagers upon the prowess of their favourite hunters soon caught on among Irish hunting-men and by 1825 regular steeplechases were being run for prizes of plates, and it was not long before the framing of various restrictions upon riders and weights elevated steeplechasing to the position of a recognised sport.

Steeplechasing made its first appearance in England in 1830 as a result of a suggestion made during a dinner by some officers of the Household Cavalry to the landlord of the Turf Hotel at St. Albans. The landlord, an astute man named Tom Coleman, saw the benefit which an annual steeplechase at St. Albans would be to him and promptly set about instituting it. His foresight was amply rewarded, for not only did he earn for himself the title of "The Father of Steeplechasing" but he also managed to add considerably to his income by letting his rooms at a guinea a night at racing time.

Of course Coleman had many imitators among the hotel-keeping fraternity, but the most successful of these was William Lynn of the Waterloo Hotel at Aintree. He, with an eye to his bank balance, entered into an arrangement with his farmer neighbours whereby they agreed to allow an annual steeplechase over their land and, on the 29th February, 1836, the first Liverpool Steeplechase was run at Maghull.

Lynn's meetings continued annually until 1839, when a syndicate was formed which purchased the racing amenities from him. This year saw at Aintree the establishment of the first proprietary course ever organised, and it was here, on the 26th February, 1839, that the Grand Liverpool Steeplechase, the first Grand National proper, was run.

The day dawned fine and spring-like, with just a slight breeze blowing up from the Mersey. The course was crowded with spectators who would look strange to our twentieth-century eyes. The men wore top-hats and frock-coats for the main part, although there would still be some who favoured the already old-fashioned Hessian boots and knee-breeches. The women were all shawls, voluminous skirts and large fan-like bonnets. The seventeen runners got off to a good start although the going was to be hard for it had been a real fill-dyke February. The race abounded in incidents. At this time the course was run over unflagged brook-studded ploughland and one of the horses, "Rust," was trapped in a lane by a hostile crowd who were determined that he should not win! Another, "Dictator," fell at the first brook, was remounted by his jockey, Carlin, only to drop dead at the next fence.

But the most famous incident of all was the christening of Becher's Brook. The gentleman whose name was bestowed on this obstacle was Captain Becher, son of a Norfolk farmer and horse-dealer. Bred in an atmosphere of horses, he was early introduced to the saddle, a position which he showed a regrettable tendency to abandon throughout his life, for he was renowned for the number and variety of his falls! He was the tumbler *par excellence*, and in many an old racing-print he is depicted in the act of falling. Becher was a member of the old school of gentlemen riders who lived the life of a professional jockey travelling from meeting to meeting, often sleeping on horseback, until his thick, curled beard (which the wags said added to his weight in the saddle) became a familiar sight to race-goers everywhere. In this first National the Captain was riding "Conrad" and as they came up to the brook at which he was to tumble into immortality the horse stumbled. Becher took a header into the water, wherein he wisely sought refuge from the flurry of skull-splintering hoofs. As soon as the danger was past, the sporting Captain sprinted after "Conrad," leapt into the saddle and set off at a cracking pace in pursuit of the field. He got as far as Valentine's Brook, where he was again thrown, and "Conrad," having had enough, made certain that the Captain should not catch him a second time!

The first man to win the Blue Riband of 'chasing was Jem Mason who rode "Lottery" first past the post in 1839. Jem was the son of a Stilton horse-jobber. He had schooled horses, including "Lottery," for John Elmore and had long dreamed of becoming a famous jockey and marrying his master's daughter with whom he was in love. He was one of the lucky ones and his dreams came true. The amazing thing about this man and the horse upon which he rode in so many Nationals is that they hated each other and Jem was always obliged to conceal his Elmore blue racing-jacket under his coat until he was mounted.

The next race was run on March 5th, 1840, and was won by "Jerry", but because of the winning of a wager made by a Mr. Power, the owner-rider of a horse named "Valentine," it is often, somewhat unfairly, referred to as "Valentine's National." For the second National, Lord Sefton had caused a new stone wall to be erected and Mr. Power had made a rather rash bet that he would be the first over it. Off went the field of twelve, "Valentine" like an arrow from the bow, thundering to the Canal Turn which he negotiated safely. But he went at the next brook as though it not been there, and it was only by a magnificent display of aerial acrobatics and the execution of a miraculous corkscrew-like twist that he managed to land on the far side of what was to be known henceforth as "Valentine's Brook." The gallant horse went on to lead the field over the new wall and win his master's wager, although he lost his lead subsequently and finished third to "Jerry".

The year 1841 is noteworthy in that the race was won for the first time by a mare, the valiant "Charity." Since then only a dozen other "remarkable ladies" have finished first in this most arduous of races: – "Miss Mowbray" (1852) , "Anatis" (1860), "Jealousy" (1861), "Emblem" (1863), "Emblematic" (1864), "Casse Tête" (1872), "Empress" (1880), "Zoedone" (1883), "Frigate" (1889), "Shannon Lass" (1902), "Sheila's Cottage" (1948) and "Nickel Coin" (1951). It is interesting to recall in passing that it was in the year of "Frigate's" win that Mrs. Maybrick and her husband had that quarrel upon the Aintree course which was among the first causes of the murder for which she later stood trial and and which became Liverpool's criminal *cause célèbre* of 1889.

In 1842 the National was won by Tom Olliver on "Gaylad." Tom Olliver was another Aintree character of the calibre of Captain Becher and Jem Mason. "Black Tom," as he was popularly called, was a native of Angmering in Sussex, who had been, in his own words "born and bred hopelessly insolvent." He was brought up by his uncle, Page of Epsom, who taught him the three R's – reading, writing and riding! When the stable passed from

Page, the young Tom went to Ireland, whence he returned to Liverpool several years later with only a few coppers in his pocket. He found a job schooling horses and eventually graduated to a jockeyship. His National career was a distinguished one. He finished second on "Seventy-Four" in the 1839 race and besides winning in 1842 he also won on "Vanguard" in 1843 and on "Peter Simple" in 1853, a record of wins exceeded only by that of George Stevens, the Grand National horseman of all time, who, from running away from his home at Cheltenham to become a stable-boy, lived to achieve the distinction of winning the National five times between 1856 and 1870. By 1855, Tom Olliver was riding in his seventeeth consecutive National and his Aintree career came to an end in 1859 when he was thrown by "Claudius" his last National mount.

Upon the eve of the race in 1847 a very curious happening took place. A clairvoyance act was in progress at a Liverpool theatre and the mediumistic lady was asked by a National-minded audience to give them the winner of the morrow's 'chase. After a suitable period of concentration the clairvoyant uttered her prophecy in favour of "Matthew." And the unbelievable happened, "Matthew" won! He was the first Irish-bred horse to win the National, which since 1900 alone has been won by more than thirty horses whose bone and substance has been built out of the rich, limestone soil of Ireland. Among the notable "foreigners" who have jumped to victory must be mentioned "Rubio" (1908) the first American-bred horse to win the National, which has since been won by another American, "Battleship," in 1938, with Bruce Hobbs up. Hobbs was, incidentally, only seventeen years old and the youngest jockey ever to taste the fruits of a National victory. France sent the 1909 winner, "Lutteur III."

The achievement of the lady fortune-seller in 1847 was certainly unique in the history of the Grand National, for it has always been, more than any other, a completely unpredictable race. Indeed, it is often and aptly described as "anybody's race!" Time and time again there have been odd and unexpected winners. Among those horses whose names are inscribed upon the equine Roll of Honour are many with the most fantastic histories. "Emigrant" (1857) was once won on a game of cards; "Salamander" (1866) was bought from a poor Irish family for £35 and won stakes to the tune of some £29,750; "Roquefort" (1855) once drew a dogcart; "Grudon" won with butter in his shoes, to prevent him from slipping in the snow in the white National of 1901; 'Rubio" (1908) had drawn an hotel bus in America; "Glenside" (1911) was a one-eyed horse; "Poethlyn" (1918 and 1919) had been sold to a publican for £17; "Master Robert" (1942) once worked in a plough, while "Tipperary Tim" (1928) won with a tube in his throat. In 1904 the laurels went to a stout-hearted horse, "Moifaa," who had swum ashore when his ship had been wrecked in British waters.

And if the stories of some of the horses seem strange, the race itself has seen many events hardly less queer in its time. Victory has repeatedly been thrown to the lucky horse by the hand of chance, and often it has been the others' lack of luck that has proved a blessing to the winner. Such was the case back in 1872 when Casse Tête won the day. Again in 1877, it was upon the wings of good fortune that "Austerlitz" won his one and only National. Some horses seem to have a natural liking for Aintree, whilst others among them the 1934 winner, "Golden Miller," hailed as the horse of the century, appear to take a strong dislike to it.

This is hardly to be wondered at, for the race is probably the most gruelling in the world. The course is a double circuit totalling 4 miles 856 yards. On the first round the horses have to clear sixteen jumps, and on the second, fourteen. The existing time record for this stiff 'chase was set by "Reynoldstown" in 1935 when he completed the course in 9 minutes 20⅕ seconds. In 1846, due to a mistake in flagging, the course was involuntarily extended to nearly five miles. This longest National ever was won by "Pioneer".

"Reynoldstown," the record-maker, is one of that elect equine company who have brought off a double victory (1935, 1936) in which he equalled the achievement of "Abd-El-Kader" (1850, 1851), "Peter Simple" (1849, 1853), "The Colonel" (1869, 1870) who was later to become Kaiser Wilhelm the First's charger, "The Lamb" (1868, 1871) the only grey ever to win the race, "Manifesto" (1897, 1899) and "Poethlyn" (1918, 1919).

Of these, "Manifesto" has earned the title of the National horse of all time, and his was a magnificent record. He was first twice, third three times, fourth once and unplaced upon one occasion. In all these Nationals he fell only once. On his second win, in 1899, he carried the top weight of 12 stone 7lbs, a feat in which he was rivalled by "Cloister" (1893), "Jerry M." (1912) and "Poethlyn" (1919).

In the earlier years, before the construction of a proper course, the size of the field offered few problems, but in later years it became necessary to devise a number of qualifying conditions upon the eligibility of would-be entrants. The greatest number of runners ever, was in 1939 when "Gregalach" won out of a field of 66 horses which had to be lined up in two rows. The smallest field was in "Zoedone's" year (1883) when there were only 10 starters. Of course the field is always considerably reduced by the end of the race and in 1882, 1921 and 1928 only two horses succeeded in completing the course. This led to the rather curious position that the last horse was also the second!

Up to 1941 the race had an unbroken history of 102 years, although during the First World War it abandoned its old home at Aintree and substitute races were run at Gatwick in 1916, 1917 and 1918. During the Second World War, however, there was no Grand National from 1941-1945.

And each year the excitement is renewed. Each year we hope that the race will be in the tradition of the fair weather Nationals and that it will not be a day of thick fog, as when "Wild Man From Borneo" (1895) won an all but invisible race by a length and a half, or a repetition of those conditions which, in 1858, saw the outsider "Little Charley" run to victory through snow and a half-gale in the National that had had to be postponed for three days.

What, we wonder, will be the name of *this* year's winner? Who has not dreamed of the infallible, magic tip such as was offered to that Liverpool audience in 1847? Yet how many of them would, for lack of faith, have failed to benefit from it? For us there remains but the abortive study of form, the loud claims of the tipsters, of whom there is a confident one for every horse in the race, or, and perhaps best of all, the ubiquitious pin!

For the winning owner there will be about £10,000, including a gold trophy valued at about £200. For the trainer of the winning horse there will be a cup valued at about £50 and for the jockey there will be a cup valued at about £25. And if, materially, his gain shall seem the least, he will not be discontented, for he will have fulfilled the greatest ambition of all 'chasing men. And in the slight pause, the breath-taking, before the glory breaks upon his head, he may find a quiet minute in which to grasp the outstretched, congratulatory hands of old Captain Becher, limping up from his latest fall, Jem Mason, Tom Olliver and a host of other ghosts whose sporting spirits surely haunt the deep shadows of the thorn hedges and hover about the ruffled waters of the brooks of their beloved legacy of earth at Aintree.

17 A POET IN DOCKLAND

Astray one summer's evening in the stilled heart of Liverpool's dockland, I spent a fruitful half-hour gazing into space. Space and time, for the portion of space which riveted my gaze was a bare plot of land at the cobbled terminus of South John Street whereon, until a decade-and-a-half ago German bombs ploughed its bricks back into the earth, there stood a tall dark warren of offices called Trafford Chambers. Sixty-eight years ago an alien songbird came to nest in the attics of that drear stronghold of nineteenth-century commerce in the person of Liverpool's greatest native poet – Richard Le Gallienne.

Richard Le Gallienne, poet, essayist, lion of the romantic nineties, and son of John Gallienne, one-time secretary of the Birkenhead Brewery Company, first saw the light of day in Everton on January 20th, 1866. Reared in Birkenhead, schooled at Liverpool College, apprenticed to accountancy in the Fenwick Street offices of Messrs. Chalmers & Wade, it was Le Gallienne's destiny to clamber out of the hated rut of life behind the dead wood of a provincial office desk. There was to be for him a brief high noon of glory as the comrade and equal of such splendid suns of *fin de siècle* London as Oscar Wilde, Aubrey Beardsley and Max Beerbohm, followed by a thirty-four-year winter of discontent in stream-lined America before, conforming to the tradition of his cohort, he returned to Europe to keep, at the age of eighty-one, a long-postponed appointment with death.

★ ★ ★ ★

It was towards the end of 1889 that Le Gallienne, having quarrelled with the rigid puritanism of his father's home, moved into the large well-lighted room which, for ten pounds a year, he rented on the seventh story of Trafford Chambers. He was to remain there little more than a year, but those twelve months were to be counted among the happiest of his whole life, and many, many times he was to look back with poignant nostalgia to that humble den at the very mast-head of that dingy building, rising high above the loftiest yards and riggings of the nearby docks, in which he "commenced author".

Le Gallienne himself has embalmed the memory of his seventh-story heaven in one of his prose fancies published in the seventh volume of that peerless nineties chronicle – *The Yellow Book*. The piece is touchingly dedicated: "For M. Le G., a Birthday Present; 25 September, 1895," and is a sad little offering to Mildred, his first wife, who had died of typhoid in May 1894, less than three years after their marriage. Richard Le Gallienne was to marry twice more, but he never really recovered from the loss of Mildred, the little blue-eyed girl, who had waited upon him at Miss MacPherson's café in

Tithebarn Street, where in his clerking days he used to go for lunch.

How good life had seemed to Richard and Mildred when, after the long climb up all those dreary flights of stairs which led from the chill region of empty, echoing offices, they opened the door which hid a gracious and strangely contrasting little world of books and flowers. Cosy behind its muslin curtains, they were free to dream: he of success as a great poet; she of becoming his wife and making a beautiful home for him and for their children. On just such nights as this the lovers would sit up there together. Sometimes Mildred would play to him upon the piano, procured with daring extravagance on hire-purchase, and softly sing, one after another, his favourite songs. At other times she would just sit quietly on the sofa watching his raven head bent over his desk as he penned page after page of his critical appreciation of George Meredith which was written in that vanished attic. And sometimes, for even poets must eat, she would cook him a meal of fried sausages, and with, if they happened to be flush, a bottle of wine between them, there they would sit, hand-in-hand, the lamp lowered, watching the stars rush down upon them through the skylight which hung above the tiny table.

Sixty-two years ago Le Gallienne wrote: "That seventh-story heaven once more leads a dull life as the office of a ship-chandler, and harsh voices grate the air where Beauty sang. The books and the flowers and the lovers' faces are gone for ever. I suppose the stars are the same, and perhaps they sometimes look down through that roof-window, and wonder what has become of those two lovers who used to look up at them so fearlessly long ago."

★ ★ ★ ★

So did I gaze, not vacantly, into space and as evening came softly over the Mersey I saw those self-same stars sequining the curtains of night. Maybe, somewhere beyond them, Richard and his Mildred were together again at last. Maybe they were looking down on this little plot of remembered earth, for surely "there is no place where a great dream has been dreamed that is not thus watched over by the guardian angels of memory."

18 THE AMATEUR GUNMAN

9.35 p.m.

March 19th, 1949.

It was just an ordinary Saturday night. The usual audience of off-duty housewives, husbands released from offices, shops and factories, and children granted a late reprieve from bedtime, were enjoying the thrilling spectacle of murder on celluloid in an unobtrusive, red-brick, Liverpool building which had once been a church and was now a suburban cinema. Shots and screams rent the air. The children delightedly sucked their lolly-ices. Their excited elders puffed hard at their cigarettes. This was the real thing! How right they were – this *was* the real thing, for in a little room away from the packed auditorium a masked man stood with a smoking pistol in his hand.

Downstairs in the staff-room of the cinema, two women employees had heard those shots and had realised that they were no part of the show. Running upstairs to see what was wrong, these two women, together with the cinema fireman, who has also heard the shots, had come face to face with a real-life murderer. A man in brown, with something dark covering the lower part of his face and a brown trilby pulled well down over his eyes, he had hesitated for a moment, and then, waving a gun in his hand, had curtly ordered them to stand back as, brushing rapidly past them, he ran out into the street.

In the manager's office at the top of the spiral staircase they found a scene of horror and chaos. The room was filled with the sharp stench of burnt cordite. The furniture was overturned. The manager and the assistant-manager lay in ever-widening pools of blood, and all about them the night's takings were scattered on the floor.

Before many minutes had elapsed an ambulance was speeding from nearby Sefton General Hospital to Webster Road and had drawn up outside the Cameo Cinema.

The manager, 39-year-old Leonard Thomas, was already dead. In the aseptic fastness of the operating theatre white-gowned surgeons fought a losing battle with death. At 11.15 p.m. the other man, John Bernard Catterall, died. Somewhere in the night their killer prowled the concrete jungle of the streets.

The problem facing the Liverpool police was a tough one. Somehow they had to identify and arrest the unknown murderer. They began by questioning those of the cinema staff who had caught a glimpse of the man on the spiral staircase. Their descriptions were necessarily vague. "A man in a belted brown overcoat. Age: 20-30. Height: about 5 feet 7 or 8 inches. Build: medium to broad." That was all. Not much to go on in a city of nearly 800,000 inhabitants. But there *was* one other thing. Something that neither the mask nor the turned-down hat could hide. All the witnesses agreed that the killer had a pair of extraordinarily dark eyebrows.

Later that night, down at the city's Dale Street police headquarters, Chief-Superintendent Tom Smith, head of the C.I.D., sent for his right-hand man, Chief Detective-Inspector H. R. Balmer. Together they studied the slender description of the wanted man. Then they went along to the criminal record department. Hour after hour the two police-officers checked, painstakingly and methodically, through the thousands of photographs and dossiers in the rogues' gallery. By the time the first pale rays of Sunday's dawn were filtering into the grey room they had decided that a certain George Kelly fitted the description. This Kelly was known as a man of violence and *he had extraordinarily dark eyebrows.*

Chief-Inspector Balmer lost no time. At 11.15 that very morning he interviewed George Kelly at the house in Cambridge Street – less than three minutes walk from the Cameo Cinema – where he was living with a woman named Doris O'Malley. But Kelly had an alibi that was to take the police 327 days to break.

"I was with James Skelly at the Coach and Horses pub just after opening time last night," said a self-confident Kelly. "He was on the booze so I left him and arranged to see him down town. He didn't turn up so I went back at 9 o'clock and saw he was drunk. I jumped a tram to the public-house opposite our street in Picton Road (the Leigh Arms) and stayed there until 10 o'clock, when I came home."

Chief-Inspector Balmer was quick to notice that although his visit was paid at a time when Kelly was usually in bed, he was not only up, but he was also dressed – and dressed fastidiously. It was obvious to him that his arrival had not been altogether unexpected. Without any hesitation, Kelly accompanied him as he set to work to check his alibi, and insisted on being present when James Skelly was interviewed. He was not present, however, when, later that day, Chief-Inspector Balmer made certain other inquiries which confirmed his suspicion that the story Kelly told of his movements was a false one. But it is one thing to know that an alibi is a fake, proving it to be so is a totally different matter, and at that stage nobody would talk. Georgie Kelly was too well known to "take liberties with."

Well that was, for the time being at any rate, a stop card. During the next six months the police visited 9,500 houses within a square mile of the Cameo Cinema, interviewed 75,000 people and seized 30 revolvers, 3 rifles and a shot-gun. The manhunt was the greatest Merseyside had ever seen, but it was utterly unproductive.

The real turning point in the case came on April 4th, 1949, when an anonymous letter was delivered to Chief-Superintendent Smith. The letter was written in carefully-printed block capitals. "Dear Sir," it began, "this letter is not a crank's letter or such like, nor am I turning informer for gain.

You have been searching Wavertree and district for the persons responsible for the death of two men killed in the cinema when the persons responsible live nowhere near where the crime was committed. It says in the papers you are looking for one man. I know three and a girl, not including myself, who heard about this plan for the robbery."

The anonymous correspondent went on to say that two men had gone to the Cameo Cinema on that fatal night, and that, under certain conditions, he was prepared to name them. "If I give my address, you may charge me with being an accessory to the killing. If you put in the personal column of the *Echo* and give me your word that I won't be charged, I will give you both their names."

After due deliberation, Chief-Superintendent Smith decided to accept the writer's conditions, and at the head of the personal column of that night's *Liverpool Echo* there appeared the enigmatic insertion "Anonymous letter received. Promise definitely given."

Weeks went by and no reply was received. Meanwhile, handwriting experts decided that the letter had been written by a woman. Night after night, bands of detectives tramped the streets of Liverpool obtaining samples of handwriting from women and girls who had been convicted or were the known associates of criminals. The search dragged on for months. Spring and summer passed, and then, as the dark nights of autumn approached, the police's persistent efforts bore fruit. One night a woman was seen, a woman whose journeyings took her all over the country. The vital question was asked and she answered that she had written the letter. What was more important, she proved that she was speaking the truth by referring to a red smudge of lipstick on the envelope. The search was over, thought the detectives – but they exulted too soon. Almost immediately, the woman disappeared again. Balmer spent weeks in Soho and other parts of London, in Bristol, Birmingham and many more big cities vainly hunting for her. It was not until late September that he traced her to Manchester and she returned with him to Liverpool. This time she did not run away, but made the statement which, together with that of her male companion, was to put the final knot in the noose around George Kelly's bull neck.

The story that Jacqueline Dickson and James 'Stutty' Northam told was a strange one. At 7.55 on the evening of March 19th, 1949, they had met Kelly and another man, named Charles Connolly, in the Beehive public-house at the bottom of Mount Pleasant. They had some drinks there and began to talk together about possible jobs.

The man Connolly spoke of premises in Islington, but the idea of breaking into them was abandoned because someone mentioned that an automatic burglar alarm was installed there. Kelly then said it might be worth trying to break into a booth at New Brighton fairground, but this was also rejected along with Connolly's proposal that they should rob a taxi driver. It was Connolly who suggested the Cameo Cinema, adding that it would have to be a stick-up job and that a gun would be needed. At this, Kelly drew a revolver out of his hip pocket. On seeing the weapon, Northam and Dickson refused to have anything to do with the robbery and, at about 8.30, after borrowing a hat and overcoat from Northam and a small brown apron to serve as a mask from a second, unnamed, woman, Kelly and Connolly caught a number 8 tram in the direction of Wavertree.

At 1 o'clock the following day the four of them met by appointment at the White Star public-house at the corner of Clarence Street and Brownlow Hill. At that meeting Kelly told Northam and Dickson that it was he who had shot Thomas and Catterall, and that Connolly, who had remained outside in the street keeping watch, had run off and left him when he heard the shooting. He also said that he was not at all worried and had a "cast-iron alibi."

Listening to the amazingly detailed account of the robbery and killings which Northam said Kelly had given him, the police knew that the time had come to pounce and, accordingly, on September 30th, George Kelly and Charles Connolly were arrested.

Kelly adopted an arrogant attitude of outraged innocence and kept on saying that he had a cast-iron alibi. Connolly contented himself with strenuous denials. He did not know George Kelly. He had never been in the Beehive. Anyway, at 9.30 on the evening of March 19th he was at a dance in St. Mark's Church Hall, Edge Lane.

The Cameo Murder Trial opened at St. George's Hall on January 12th, 1950, before Mr. Justice Oliver. For thirteen drama-packed days a long procession of 68 witnesses gave their evidence before a court that was crowded to capacity. Gradually the pieces fitted together. The whole sordid story took shape. The prosecution shattered Kelly's cast-iron alibi into a thousand fragments. And then, on the thirteenth and final day of the longest murder trial in British criminal history . . . the jury disagreed. After an absence of 4 hours and 8 minutes the foreman admitted that there was no hope of their reaching agreement, and the judge had no option but to order a re-trial.

But for Connolly at least, the ordeal was over, for when the second trial opened before Mr. Justice Cassels on February 2nd, 1950, Kelly stood alone in the dock. Charles Connolly had elected to plead guilty to a charge of robbery, in respect of which he was sentenced, on February 13th, 1950, to ten years' imprisonment.

Kelly's second trial lasted six days. This time the jury was not divided. They were out a mere 55 minutes before returning an uncompromising 'Guilty'.

On March 28th, 1950, just one year and nine days after he had brutally murdered two men in a suburban cinema, George Kelly paid with his own life on the scaffold at Walton Gaol. He was only twenty-seven when he died, but his career had been an evil one. From small beginnings in crime when, at the age of eleven, he had been put on probation for school-breaking and larceny, he had graduated through a number of petty offences to his first taste of prison. That was in December 1943 when he received nine months for kicking a pregnant woman in the stomach and rupturing her bladder. Oddly enough, the judge who sent him to prison on that occasion was Mr. Justice Cassels who was later to sentence him to death. His war record was equally unsavoury. On September 28th, 1945, he was discharged from the Royal Navy and sentenced by a court-martial to three years' penal servitude in respect of five charges of desertion.

It was in the slightly feverish atmosphere of post-war Liverpool, however, that Kelly really blossomed forth. He was a little man who loved to act big, and when he was not helping his mother to hawk fruit on her barrow, or acting as barker to the escapologist on the blitzed site at the corner of Ranelagh Street, he liked to make a big splash in the small drinking-pools of the town. "My name's Kelly," he used to boast. "Nobody takes liberties with Kelly." I met him myself and had a glass or two of beer with him. I found him quite amiable, but in the bars and cafés under the bright lights of Lime Street he was a force to be reckoned with. They used to call him the Little Caesar of Lime Street and, surrounded by his fawning mob of strongarm boys, he saw himself as the sleek well-dressed gang boss of the screen. When he planned the big armed robbery that was to justify himself in his own eyes, it was pathetically in character that he should choose a tiny suburban cinema – and make a hash even of that. Still, he got his little hour of fame in the end, and the man who loved to impress had an audience of more than a thousand people waiting in the street outside St. George's Hall to hear that he had been condemned to death.

19 COSSETING THE CALDER STONES

I have just been to the Cleansing Department Yard in Garston Old Road to see the earliest example of man's handiwork on Merseyside – some 4,000-year-old stone-carvings.

An official lifted the edge of a huge tarpaulin, and there, prone upon the cobbles, lay six great slabs of sandstone which have, for the last 109 years, stood at the entrance to Calderstones Park, marking the junction of three townships.

First mentioned in the year 1568, when they were cited as an undisputed boundary point during a territorial disagreement between the Manors of Allerton and Wavertree, the Calder Stones have been an enigma to the autochthonous Merseysider for close on 400 years. In mediaeval times, an ignorant peasantry inclined to the view that they were somehow connected with witchcraft, a belief which may well have originated with the Saxons, for one interpretation of the complex etymology of the word *Calders* is that it stems from the Anglo-Saxon *Gualder* which means a wizard or warlock. This notion persisted for centuries, until, in fact, Stukeley and other disciples of romantic eighteenth-century antiquarian fervour initiated the cult of the Druid, when the Calder Stones came to be regarded as a "Druidical Circle," and queasy folk of archaeological bent professed to see in them a sacrificial temple redolent of mistletoe, golden sickles and runnelled altar-stones disgustingly besmirched with the blood of human sacrifices! A quaint conception enshrined to this day in the name of the nearby district of Druids Cross.

Informed twentieth-century opinion, derived from the painstaking researches of modern science, has substituted for this lurid legend a less bloody, though in no respect less wonderful, history, which has the additional advantage of accuracy.

The clue to the real nature of the Calder Stones is to be found in certain ancient records. In 1896, a local antiquary, E. W. Cox, related how his gardener, Robert Peers (1801-1887), who had worked on Calderstones Farm as a boy, remembered the stones being partially buried in a large mound of sand. From various sources it appears that although at one time only small portions of some of the stones were visible protruding from the top of this little hillock, between 1760 and 1790 much of the sand was carted away by builders. By 1805, the mound had been so severely diminished that it collapsed, and, in 1815, it was entirely removed when the road was widened. After that, the stones lay neglected on the farm until the illustrious William Roscoe of Allerton Hall had them set up in a "Druids' Circle." Subsequently, in 1845, the circle was enclosed, by the order of Joseph Need Walker of Calderstone House, within a low stone wall surmounted by stout railings.

This planting of the stones in a ring was very misleading for it suggested that they had originally formed a cromlech – a kind of miniature Stonehenge. This was not so, for the evidence of early descriptions makes it abundantly clear that the Calder Stones made up a stone burial-chamber bedded in a tumulus of the type which present-day archaeologists call a barrow.

These barrows occur all over Britain and in many other parts of the world. The conspicuous manner in which they hug the coastline from Land's End to Orkney, and cluster about inland waterways which connect with the sea, suggests that they are the work of a maritime people who made the Atlantic and the Irish Sea their highways. They are generally attributed to the Iberians, an advanced group of Mediterranean folk, ultimately deriving from Egypt, whose unity was one of strong religious tradition. Their religion has been termed *Megalithic* (Greek. Big Stone) because one of its chief tenets lay in the construction of big stone monuments, the vast majority of which were funerary in function.

In all Near East and Mediterranean centres of civilisation – particularly in Egypt – vast labours and wealth were expended upon the dead in order to secure their contentment in the next world and, the cynic might hazard, to ensure their continued goodwill towards their survivors. In rocky districts inhumation in natural caves or rock-cut sepulchres was the custom: where, however, no rock occurred, stone tombs had to be built. The pyramids themselves are nothing more than gigantic artificial caves. When, perhaps in search of *lebensraum,* the Iberians set out upon their migrations, they took their megalithic ideals with them and scattered innumerable examples of their Cyclopean architecture in their wake. All these, despite the emergence of several distinct traditions as a result of local schisms, display a sufficiently strict agreement in arbitrary detail to make them as reliable witnesses of megalithic religion as are mosques for Mohammedanism.

After about 2,500 B.C., men raised such monuments in Sicily, Sardinia, Southern France, Spain and Portugal. From these centres the practice extended to Brittany, to our own coasts and onwards to the shores of the Baltic, until, at the end of 500 years, the megaliths pointed like Gargantuan milestones the progress of the navigators in little dug-out canoes, past Gibraltar, across the Bay of Biscay and right up to Sweden.

The Calder Stones, which by the way were situated less than two miles in direct line from the coast, probably represent colonisation by Megalithic Iberians via Ireland, and belong to the same art tradition as the circular chambered-tomb of Bryn Celli Dhu at Anglesey and the cruciform chambered-tomb of Barclodiad y Gawres. All three were nothing more or less than carefully contrived mausoleums. They vary in structural details it is true, but architectural differences do not necessarily reflect differences in faith, for does not the tin Bethel preach the same gospel as the cruciform cathedral? Each barrow was built as a family vault to shelter the remains of a chief and those of the members of his family. The Megalithic burial-ritual seems to have been fairly complicated. In the British Isles cremation was the normal rite, and in the case of the Calder Stones the discovery of several coarse clay cinerary-urns containing quantities of calcined human bones, confirms its practice. It is easy to imagine the scene. A great chieftain was dead; he had passed into the land of his fathers. Amidst the wailings and lamentations of his people the hallowed corpse would be carried to some spot close to the grave it was to occupy. Perhaps a tall wooden funeral-pyre had been erected, and the body was placed reverently upon its summit. The high-priest or holy man of the tribe would then set the great pile alight and its flickering flames would soon flare up, consuming the corpse and silhoutteing the queer, skin-clad figures of the mourners against the horizon. As the last flames died down, the charred bones would be gathered from the smouldering heap, scooped into a special urn, and, to the accompaniment of mystic chanting and incantations, be placed in the dark rock-cavern which had been prepared for them.

Upon the surfaces of the Calder Stones there occur certain carvings in the form of spirals, concentric circles and so-called cup-and-ring markings. Their significance is obscure, but they were probably religious symbols connected with the magical aspect of the burial-ritual and very likely disclose the chthonic deity to whose bosom the faithful dead hoped to return. In any event they are invaluable, numbering among the first important efforts at non-representational art in western Europe, and constituting the sole expression of serious decorative purpose prior to the advent of the beautiful secular art of the Celts nearly 2,000 years later. Moreoever, they establish an informative link with the great Hibernian megalithic monument of New Grange, Co. Meath, Ireland, which is situated almost directly opposite Liverpool on the other side of the Irish Sea, and upon which identical markings are present.

It was concern for the fate of these carvings on the Calder Stones which, in November 1952, worried Mr. J. H. Iliffe, director of the Liverpool Museum. After carrying out an examination and test excavation, he said that the markings were deteriorating due to weather-erosion, and proposed that they should be removed from their exposed site on Menlove Avenue. Accordingly, one September morning in 1954, nine men with a mobile crane and a low-loader set about removing the stones. It was no easy task, for the largest stone weighed more than 3 tons and even the smallest was a burden of 4 or 5 cwt. However, the job was accomplished in a single day, and, carefully wrapped in sacking, the stones were transported to the Corporation Yard where they now lie.

I talked with Mr. J. J. Forde-Johnston, the archaeologist who is coping with the detailed examination of the stones. Sitting at his desk in a room in Carnatic Hall which was littered with dusty adzes and flints and looked, in the blood-orange light of the November afternoon sunshine, like a prehistoric armoury, he told me of his work on the Calder Stones. Apparently, the cleansing yard is an appropriate place for them, for the stones are in a very bad state. Even the atmosphere of Liverpool's green belt seems to be none too pure, for it has stained them as black as jet. Mr. Forde-Johnston had already set to work cleaning them with a toothbrush! He had also begun to paint them with a green solution of latex rubber which takes very adequate impressions of the carvings. On a nearby work-table I saw a series of careful scale-drawings which were being completed and which will record for posterity all the markings, including any which may be discovered on portions of the stones hitherto buried in the ground.

The ultimate fate of the Calder Stones still hangs in the balance. Some people would like to see them housed under cover in the museum and artificial stone replicas erected at the entrance to Calderstones Park. But whatever decision is eventually reached, we may be sure that it will be to preserve Liverpool's 4,000-year-old heritage, for a wise committee of city fathers is well aware of their unique importance and is fully determined to cosset the Calder Stones.